PIER World Education Series

Central America Update

An Update of the 1987 PIER Workshop Report on the Systems and Institutions of Higher Education in Belize, Costa Rica, El Salvador, Guatemala, Honduras, Nicaragua, and Panama

Special

Report

1996

Jane E. Marcus

A Projects for International Education Research (PIER) Publication sponsored by the American Association of Collegiate Registrars and Admissions Officers, NAFSA: Association of International Educators, and The College Board

Washington, DC

Library of Congress Cataloging-in-Publication Data

Marcus, Jane E.
  Central America Update : an update of the 1987 PIER Workshop Report on the
Systems and Institutions of Higher Education in Belieze, Costa Rica, El Salvador,
Guatemala, Honduras, Nicaragua, and Panama : Special Report 1996 / Jane E. Marcus
        p.   cm. -- (PIER world education series)
Update of: The admission and placement of students from Central America. 1987.
  "A Projects for International Education Research (PIER) publication sponsored by
the American Association of Collegiate Registrars and Admissions Officers/AACRAO,
NAFSA/Association of International Educators, and The College Board."
  Includes bibliographical references and index.
  ISBN 0-929851-76-5
  1. Education, Higher--Central America. 2. School grade placement--United States.
3. College credits--United States. I. Marcus, Jane E. (Jane Elizabeth, 1961-   . II.
American Association of Collegiate Registrars and Admissions Officers. III. NAFSA:
Association of International Educators (Washington, D.C.) IV. Projects for International
Education Research (U.S.) V. College Entrance Examination Board. VI. Admission
and placement of students from Central America. VII. Series: World education series.

LA438.C46 1987
370'.9728--dc20   95-43818

American Association of Collegiate Registrars
and Admissions Officers
One Dupont Circle, Suite 330
Washington, DC 20036-1171
TEL: 202/293-9161 FAX: 202/872-8857

NAFSA: Association of International Educators
1875 Connecticut Avenue, Suite 1000
Washington, DC 20009-5728
TEL: 202/462-4811 FAX: 202/667-3419

The American Association of Collegiate Registrars and Admissions Officers, founded in 1910, is a nonprofit, voluntary professional education association of degree-granting postsecondary institutions, government agencies, private educational organizations, and education-oriented businesses. Its goal is to promote higher education and further the professional development of members working in admissions, enrollment management, financial aid, institutional research, records, and registration.

NAFSA: Association of International Educators is a nonprofit membership association that provides training, information, and other educational services to professionals in the field of international educational exchange. Its 6,500 members, from the United States and more than 50 countries, make it the largest professional membership association concerned with the advancement of effective international educational exchange in the world.

Copies of this and other volumes in the World Education Series may be obtained by contacting PIER Programs (202/462-4811). Ordering information and a list of currently available PIER publications can be found on the last pages of this book.

Contents

Illustrations

Projects for International Education Research Committee

AACRAO Members
Chair: William H. Smart, Director of Sponsored Student Programs, International Education, Oregon State University, Corvallis, OR
Margery J. Ismail, Director Emerita of International Student Services, Purdue University, West Lafayette, IN
Sylvia K. Higashi, Assistant Dean, College of Continuing Education and Community Service, University of Hawaii at Manoa, Honolulu, HI

NAFSA Members
Kathleen Sellew, Research and Professional Development, Office of International Education, University of Minnesota, Minneapolis, MN
Patricia Parker, Assistant Director of Admissions, Iowa State University, Ames, IA
Cynthia Fish, Assistant Director of Admissions, CUNY-Baruch College, New York, NY

The College Board Member
Sanford C. Jameson, Director, International Education Office, The College Board, Washington, DC

Ex-Officio Members Without Vote
AACRAO-Wayne E. Becraft, Executive Director, AACRAO, Washington, DC
NAFSA-Naomi Collins, Executive Vice President & CEO, NAFSA: Association of International Educators, Washington, DC

Observers
Agency for International Development-Dale E. Gough, Director, AACRAO-AID/Office of International Education Services, Washington, DC
United States Information Agency-Mary Reeber, Chief, Advising and Student Services Branch, Office of Academic Programs, USIA, Washington, DC

Staff
AACRAO-Henrianne K. Wakefield, Assistant Executive Director Communications, AACRAO, Washington, DC
NAFSA-Linda H. Callihan, Program Manager, Field Services; Jeanne-Marie Duval, Senior Director, Educational Programs, NAFSA: Association of International Educators, Washington, DC

This volume in the World Education Series (WES) is a Special Report update of a PIER Workshop Report (1987) on the *Admission & Placement of Students from Central America,* a study of the structure and content of the postsecondary educational systems of Central America. Each WES volume is published in accordance with standards of independent academic research and does not seek to advance any domestic or international political aim.

The World Education Series is published by PIER (Projects for International Education Research), a committee of appointed representatives from the American Association of Collegiate Registrars and Admissions Officers (AACRAO), NAFSA: Association of International Educators, and The College Board. PIER was formed in 1990 with the merger of two long-standing committees: the World Education Series Committee of AACRAO and the PIER Committee of AACRAO and NAFSA. The members of the PIER Committee during the research and development of this volume are listed on the opposite page.

PIER is charged with research and dissemination of information on educational systems throughout the world, for use in the admission and placement of students and scholars in educational institutions in the United States. In addition to publishing reports on these systems, PIER develops workshops and seminars on international credentials evaluation.

Four types of publications make up the World Education Series: full country studies, workshop reports, special reports, and working papers. The PIER Committee oversees the selection of topics, authors, and reviewers. Among the topics covered are levels of education, institutions, admission and program requirements, grading systems, credentials awarded, and study abroad programs. Placement recommendations, when included, are approved by the National Council on the Evaluation of Foreign Educational Credentials. For more information concerning the National Council and its members, see page 124. Information and an order form for currently available PIER volumes can be found on the last two pages of this book.

Kathleen Sellew, Chair

Acknowledgments

This report was written while I was working for the Central American Program of Undergraduate Scholarships (CAMPUS), a Fulbright program sponsored by the United States Information Agency and administered by the Latin American Scholarship Program of American Universities (LASPAU). As LASPAU officers, my colleagues and I observed the "boom" in Central American institutions, most notably in the number and range of private postsecondary programs throughout the region. Since we were working closely with Central American students and their home institutions through the exchange programs, it seemed logical that we would undertake the task of updating the original PIER Workshop Report.

Most of the information was obtained through visits to the institutions, although we also relied upon assistance from the Central American staff members at the United States Information Service (USIS) posts in-country. I am especially grateful to these professionals, who have dedicated their careers to the improvement of educational opportunities for their fellow Central Americans. They were: Marie Gabb (Belize), Ana Lucia de Salas and Shirley Brenes (Costa Rica), Jorge Piche (El Salvador), Carmen de Foncea (Guatemala), Karla Castañeda (Honduras), Maira Vargas and Marisela Quintana (Nicaragua), and Belsi de Medina (Panama). They each offered a wealth of information about their country's educational systems and provided invaluable advice and assistance for this project.

In Central America, numerous people supplied information about their institutions and offered insight into their countries' educational systems. I wish to give special thanks to the following individuals: Alvaro Rosado, Dorian Barrow, Angel Cal, Herman Byrd, Brian Candler, Janet Hernandez, and Adrian Leiva (Belize); Manuel M. Murillo, Pablo Arce, Ligia Rivas, Joaquín Jiménez, and Carlos Salas Arias (Costa Rica); Luís Reyes, Margarito Calderón, and Miguel Aguilar (El Salvador); Leopoldo Colóm Molina and Maria Regina Recinos Leal (Guatemala); Victor Leva, Norma Cecilia Martín de Reyes, Ana Licona, and Elio David Alvarenga Amador (Honduras); Marisela Quintana (Nicaragua); Stanley Muschett, Lesbia de Espino, and Antonio Dominguez (Panama). To the many more people who contributed information and filled out questionnaires, but whose names do not appear here, please accept my apologies and my gratitude for your assistance. This report could not have been written without you.

This project was also created with the assistance of my colleagues at LASPAU. LASPAU is a nonprofit organization affiliated with Harvard University, which designs, develops, and implements exchange programs on behalf of individuals and institutions in the Americas. Its commitment to

Latin America is unique among educational exchange organizations; its hard-working staff is highly dedicated to the LASPAU mission. The LASPAU travelers to Central America -- Ronald Berg, Winthrop Carty, and Maggie Hug -- gathered much of the documentation included in this report and supported the project throughout its gestation period. Their combined expertise on Central America spans several decades and I was fortunate to have worked with them during my LASPAU years.

The original PIER report was written by two dozen U.S. and Canadian international exchange experts, and edited by Kathleen Sellew (formerly of LASPAU and currently of the University of Minnesota), and Caroline Aldrich-Langen (of California State University at Chico). It has been a humbling experience to follow in their footsteps in the update of their 1987 report. They have been constructive with their advice and generous in their support of this effort; it has been a great learning process to work with them. I am especially grateful and indebted to Taylor Gregg for his editorial support and guidance in bringing this project to completion. I would also like to acknowledge Liz Reisberg, author of the original El Salvador chapter, for her useful assistance.

This project has been a labor of love. It was inspired by the hundreds of Central American students whose desire for knowledge overcomes every barrier: economic, political, linguistic, and cultural, and the administrators and educators who help make their dreams come true. In an era of peace and improving relations among the American nations, it is a pleasure to contribute to our understanding of the educational possibilities available to our neighbors.

Finally, research such as this report, which relies on information that is constantly changing, depends upon the support of colleagues to remain relevant. With your input, suggestions, and updates, this can be a "work-in-progress," that continues to evolve and improve through time. To the institutions and/or programs that were inadvertently excluded, I invite you to contact me with current information. As long as this dialogue remains open, all of us in the international education community can benefit immeasurably.

Jane E. Marcus
c/o Latin American Studies Program
Paul H. Nitze School of Advanced International Studies (SAIS)
Johns Hopkins University
1740 Massachusetts Ave., NW
Washington, D.C. 20036
jmarcus@igc.apc.org

Jane Marcus is a doctoral candidate in international relations and Latin American Studies at the Paul H. Nitze School of Advanced International Studies (SAIS) of Johns Hopkins University, and an associate at the Inter-American Dialogue. She was previously a project officer at the Latin American Scholarship Program of American Universities (LASPAU), working with the Fulbright Central American Program of Undergraduate Scholarships. Jane has lived, worked, and studied in Nicaragua, Argentina, and Mexico, and has traveled extensively throughout Latin America. She holds a master's degree from SAIS and a bachelor's degree from the University of Chicago.

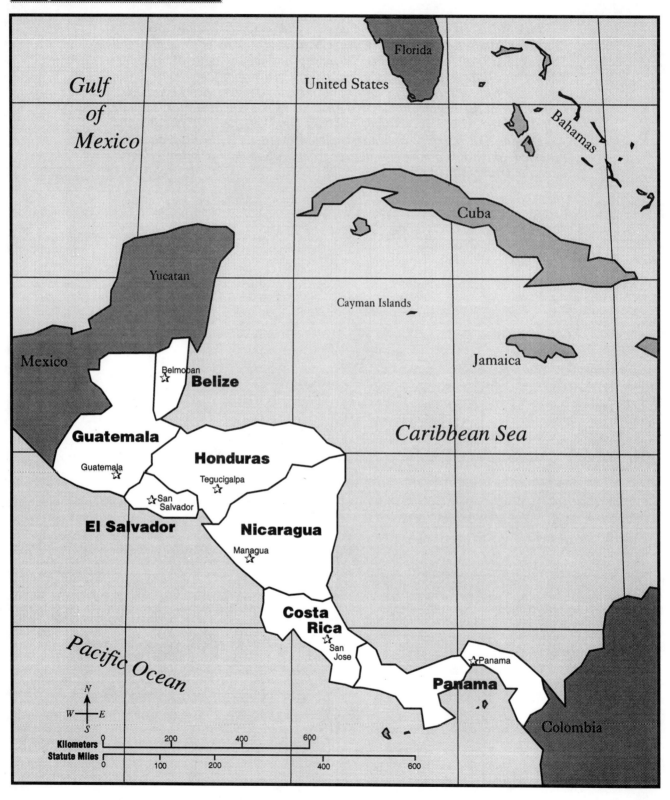

Gulf
of
Mexico

Florida

United States

Bahamas

Cuba

Yucatan

Cayman Islands

Mexico

Belmopan
☆
Belize

Jamaica

Caribbean Sea

Guatemala

Guatemala
☆

Honduras

Tegucigalpa
☆

☆ San
Salvador

El Salvador

Nicaragua

Managua
☆

**Costa
Rica**

San
☆ Jose

☆ Panama

Panama

Colombia

Pacific Ocean

N
W—E
S

Kilometers
0   200   400   600

Statute Miles
0   100   200   400   600

Chapter 1
Introduction

In 1987, 24 professionals in international education administration traveled to Central America to conduct research on the region's educational systems. The result was *The Admission and Placement of Students from Central America: A PIER Workshop Report*, (Caroline Aldrich-Langen and Kathleen Sellew, eds., Washington: National Association of Foreign Student Affairs, 1987) a comprehensive guide that has, since its publication, become the standard reference for admissions officers, study abroad personnel, and others working in international educational exchanges. It continues to serve as an invaluable reference, and this report would not presume to replace it.

Why An Update?

Central America has changed dramatically since the 1980s, economically, politically, and ideologically, and as a result, its systems of higher education have changed with the times. The 1980s represented a decade of violence and war for several countries, Nicaragua and El Salvador for example, and intense U.S. interest and involvement, as witness the 1989 invasion of Panama. The end of the Cold War, a decade of debt, free trade policies, and pressures for privatization, have all added to an international boom in technology and the media. The result is a contemporary Central America with a very different face. While the 1980s were marked by a strong military presence in government, accompanied by high levels of civic unrest, the present-day nations of the region all have democratically-elected governments and, most important, relative peace.

In higher education, the 1990s have witnessed a proliferation of private postsecondary institutions in most Central American countries. The large public universities still dominate higher education in nearly every nation, and their programs have multiplied in content and number. Teaching about the environment, tourism, and business administration, as well as computer science, has become *de rigueur* at public and most private institutions. Another trend, which appears to be part of a global phenomenon, is that funding for public education is extremely tight. As one consequence, the salaries of instructors have suffered considerably and many faculty members now hold positions at two or more universities. Regional economic pressures have also limited access to higher education, with the poorest inhabitants either excluded from the system or hindered in their educational options. Many students who manage to enter the universities but cannot complete their studies withdraw for economic reasons.

This report will not devote itself to the socioeconomic context of higher education in Central America. Readers would be well-advised to consult available sources to gain insight into the social, military, cultural, and linguistic situations of the isthmus nations. It is important to note that in relatively poor countries such as those discussed in this report, access to education, economic and political conditions, and at times military conflicts, play a key role in the quality of the population's educational development.

Methodology

The preparation of this report reflects the economic, technological, and logistical realities of international educational research today. Unlike the original guide, which involved two dozen researchers traveling to Central America, there was no such organized mission to update the report. While some documentation was obtained during travels to the region, technology greatly facilitated much of the process.

Gathering information in developing countries can be especially challenging. First, since many Central American postsecondary institutions do not have written catalogs that include all of their programs of study or credentials awarded, we developed a questionnaire and requested that administrators provide the necessary statistics and program descriptions. While these questionnaires were generally transmitted by fax machine (although not every institution has a fax machine, they usually have access to one in the area), and arrived immediately, there was frequently a lag in receiving responses. However, once the questionnaires were returned, the information about the institution was relatively complete.

Another effective tool used was electronic mail. While not every administrator in Central America is connected to the Internet, there is someone in every country (usually at a university or binational center), who has an e-mail address. From Punta Gorda, Belize to Managua, Nicaragua, we obtained information for this guide electronically. As this technology can only expand and improve, it is highly recommended for this type of research.

International students can also provide a wealth of information about education in their home countries. We spoke with numerous current and former Fulbright grantees who shared valuable first-hand knowledge. They also have great contacts at home; one student had his friend in Panama gather study plans from the national university and forward them to us for the report! In many countries, there are also Fulbright alumni associations, which can usually be contacted through the U.S. embassy. Their members are scholars who have studied in the United States and in their home countries, and can provide information in a comparative perspective.

Finally, there are four key elements to conducting research of this type: language, cross-cultural skills, creativity, and patience. Knowing the language and familiarizing oneself with the culture to be studied are fundamental. In Central America, with the exception of Belize, only a small percentage of educational materials are translated into English. Language skills are fundamental, as is general information about life in the country being examined. For example, if most students work full time and attend university classes in the evening or on the weekends (as is the case in Guatemala), this should be considered in viewing their credentials. If students have studied in zones of military conflict, or if the universities are frequently closed for economic reasons or civil unrest, these factors also influence the students' educational experiences. The final two elements (creativity and patience) are self-explanatory and must be constantly kept in mind when conducting research anywhere, but especially in a developing country.

Central Americans at U.S. Colleges and Universities:

The purpose of this guide, ultimately, is to assist professionals in international education to obtain up-to-date information about higher education in Central America. In 1992/93, international enrollments at U.S. colleges and universities totaled 438,618. Approximately 10 percent of them (43,250) came from Latin America. While the number represents a slight decline in numbers from the previous year, the quantity of Central Americans went from 12,820 in 1991/92 to 13,460 in 1992-1993. They now make up 31 percent of the Latin American total. Two-thirds of the Central Americans come to the United States for undergraduate studies, with Panama sending the highest proportion at that level. The largest number of graduate students from the region are Costa Ricans, at 44 percent. (Source: *Open Doors*, 1992-1993).

The 1987 PIER Report

The update does not replace the 1987 PIER Report on Central America. Where pertinent information must be repeated, the original report is cited and should be consulted for a complete explanation and background information concerning the topic.

The report does not make placement recommendations. The original workshop authors toiled through the arduous task of comparing Central American credentials with those from the United States. These recommendations generally continue to be valid. The actual credentials awarded in the region have changed very little; updates are noted as such.

Finally, and perhaps most importantly, this is a guide to academic programs offered at Central American postsecondary institutions. Primary, secondary, and most technical programs are generally not addressed, nor are many foreign-based institutions operating in the region described. Again, the reader would be well-served by consulting the original PIER Report. It continues to be the most comprehensive reference available for this information.

Chapter 2
The Educational System of Belize

The Country

Belize celebrated its first decade of independence from Great Britain in 1991. In education, as in cultural and economic ties, it has increasingly divided its alliances and models between its former colonizer and the United States. And, while Belizeans maintain their status as an English-speaking Caribbean country on the Central American isthmus, their neighbors are also playing a stronger role in Belizean demographics.

A tiny tropical country, Belize is bordered to the north by Mexico and to the west by Guatemala, with the Caribbean Sea on the East. It boasts the second largest coral reef in the world, and significant Mayan ruins, which have been a key factor in bringing about a recent boom in tourism. This international interest in Belize has spilled over into the classroom, where courses in eco-tourism and environmental issues are emerging in curricula. Belize, one of the least densely populated countries in the world, and a convenient stop-over between South and North America, is also finding itself caught up in hemispheric drug trafficking and its accompanying legal and social effects.

The People

With its population hovering at just under 200,000, Belize's inhabitants are a linguistic, racial, and ethnic rainbow. Creoles, who are primarily descendants of African slaves, make up approximately 40 percent of the population. They are concentrated in Belize City, and speak Creole (a dialectic form of English).

It is generally estimated that Spanish-speaking *mestizos* form one-third to one-half of Belize's inhabitants (the 1990 census indicated that Belize's population is 28 percent Creole and 43 percent *mestizo*). According to World Bank and U.S. State Department statistics, Spanish is the native tongue of about 50 percent of the population and is spoken as a second language by another 20 percent.

Ten percent of Belizeans are Amerindians, 7 percent are Garifuna, and Caucasians (generally U.S. or British) constitute about 4 percent. There is also a minority of

Official name: Belize
Area: 22,963 square kilometers/8,866 square miles
(slightly larger than Massachusetts)
Capital: Belmopan
Population: Approximately 200,000
Annual growth rate: About 8 percent, due to high
immigration rate
Noun and adjective: Belizean(s)
Ethnic groups: Creole, African, Mestizo, Amerindian.
Religions: Catholic, Anglican, Methodist, Muslim,
Buddhist, and other Protestant
Languages: English (official), Spanish, Mayan
Education: Years compulsory-9; Attendance-55
percent; Literacy - more than 80
percent

(Source: U.S. State Department *Background Notes*, 1992)

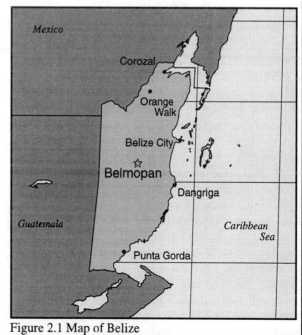

Figure 2.1 Map of Belize

East Indians, and a sizable Mennonite sect concentrated in the Cayo and Orange Walk Districts.

The Language

The 1987 PIER Workshop report distinguishes Belize from the other Central American nations as the region's only predominantly English-speaking country. English is still the official and most common language in Belize, but Spanish, Garifuna, and Mayan dialects are also heard widely. Of increasing prominence is a hybrid of English and Spanish Creole, heard in everyday usage.

The Spanish-speaking mestizo population lives mainly in northern Belize, near Mexico. Although heavily concentrated in the Corozal District, the language of instruction in all Belizean schools, including the sixth form and junior colleges, remains English.

The Future

As Spanish speakers continue to immigrate into Belize, the English-speaking Creoles are emigrating into the United States and other countries. It is estimated that 25 percent of the Belizean population lives in the United States. If present migratory trends continue, English speakers may be a minority in Belize in the future. Programs in bilingual education and English as a Second Language (ESL) are beginning to appear, especially in the Spanish-dominated parts of the country. However, there is no apparent plan on the part of the government (which continues to be dominated by English speakers), to accommodate the needs of Spanish speakers in higher education. Even with these demographic changes, it is important to emphasize that education in Belize is uniformly taught in English, and all students are either English-speaking, fully bilingual, or multilingual.

Postsecondary Education

Belize has increased its ties to the United States in recent years, economically, politically, and culturally. Having passed over a decade since its independence, the country has, in effect, created a parallel educational system to accommodate both its traditional British structures and a U.S. higher education model. For example, the emphasis on CXC and GCE exams has declined in Belize in recent years, and in many cases students may opt for either an associate degree track or an "A level" track, or an option that will give both an associate degree and "A level" results. Some associate degree programs are based on "A level" curricula and some are not. Please refer to the 1987 PIER Report for details. For example, even though a student may choose the "A level"-based associate degree program, the student can receive the associate degree without sitting for the "A level" examinations.

Many postsecondary programs require either "O level" passes for admission, or, increasingly, the U.S.-based ACT exam. The grading system and academic calendar also match those of the United States.

Perhaps the most important recent development in Belizean postsecondary education is the emergence of the University College of Belize (UCB), the first bachelor's degree-granting institution in the country. To complement its programs, the UCB has established Belmopan Junior College in the nation's capital, bringing the total number of postsecondary institutions in Belize to ten. These include Belize Teachers' College, Belize Technical College, Belize School of Nursing, Belize College of Agriculture, Corozal Junior College, Stann Creek Ecumenical College, St. John's College, Muffles College Sixth Form, Belmopan Junior College, and the UCB.

Several associations have been established to coordinate standards in higher education and to monitor the quality of Belizean colleges. The most prominent consortia are the Association of Tertiary Level Institutions and the Consortium for Belizean Educational Cooperation (COBEC). However, credential-granting authority and institutional recognition continue to lie in the hands of the central Ministry of Education.

External Examinations

As a former British colony with traditionally stronger ties to the Caribbean Commonwealth than to its Spanish-speaking neighbors, Belize continues to participate in the Caribbean Examinations Council (CXC). The Council administers two types of external examinations, commonly referred to as the General Certificate of Education Ordinary Level examinations ("O level" exams), and the General Certificate of Education Advanced Level examinations (the "A level" exams). "O level" exams are given to students upon completion of secondary school, and results are frequently used as admissions criteria for postsecondary programs. After students have completed the first 2 years of postsecondary studies, they may opt to take the GCE "A level" exams. In British-based systems, students spend the first 2 years of postsecondary studies as a university preparation cycle. However, in the Belizean hybrid of this system, these years are designed to conform to the U.S.-style associate degree track that students may complete with 2 years of postsecondary coursework.

As noted above, the number of students opting for the "A level" exams after completing a 2-year postsecondary institution has been steadily decreasing. As students shift their focus from continuing their education with postsecondary studies in Great Britain to opportunities in the United States, the external examinations have diminished in importance. However, the British term for 2-year postsecondary programs, (the "sixth form") continues to be the name for such programs. Belizeans use the terms "sixth form" and "junior college" almost interchangeably. Students earn an associate degree upon completion of the programs.

It is also important to understand that high school or secondary programs in Belize can be referred to as "community colleges." A student may proceed to Corozal <u>Junior</u> College following graduation from Corozal <u>Community</u> College. (See, for example, Document 2.1)

Institutional Profiles

BELCAST (Belize College of Arts, Science, and Technology)

(Dismantled in 1986) Note: BELCAST's records are housed at the University College of Belize.

Belize College of Agriculture
(formerly Belize School of Agriculture)

Central Farm

Cayo District
Belize

- **Organization:** The Belize College of Agriculture, so named in 1986, offers a 2-year associate degree in agriculture. The school year runs from September to July, and is divided into three 13-week terms. Its emphasis is on "hands-on" field training and many students participate in practical internships during the summer.

- **Grading System:** Grades range from A-F, on a 4-point scale. At the College of Agriculture, 1 credit hour equals 1 lecture hour per week. A lecture hour lasts fifty minutes.

Table 2.1 Belize College of Agriculture, Associate Degree Course

Year I		Year II	
Term I	Lecture Hrs./Week	Term I	Lecture Hrs./Week
Biology I	3	Crops - Sugar cane/ rice	2
Chemistry 1	2	- Plant pest mgmt.	3
Math / Measurement	2	- Weed Science	3
Agrometeorology	1	Livestock- Beef Cattle	3
Communication	2	- Small stock &	
Principles of Crop Husbandry	2	horse management	3
Plant Propagation	2	- Veterinary Practioner	2 + 1
Farm Mechanization	3	Principles of Watershed	
		Management	3
TOTAL	20		20

Term II		Term II	
Biology II	3	Crops - Semi Perm/Fruit	3
Chemistry II	2	- Plant Disease Mgmt.	3
Land Survey and Leveling	1	Livestock- Pigs	3
Communication II	2	Practices of Watershed Management	3
Crops - Corn/Sorghum/Beans	3	Crop Storage Technology	3
Livestock - Poultry	3	Agriculture Economics I	3
- Apiculture	3	Forestry	2
Farm Mechanization II	3		
TOTAL	20		20

Term III		Term III	
Biology II	2	Crops - Oil Seeds	2
Biology IV	2	- Coffee and Cacao	2
Agricultural Statistics	2	Food Processing Technology	3
Soils and Fertilizers	3	Meat and Hide Technology	3
Crops- Vegetable/Roots Crops	3	Agriculture Economics II	3
- Pasture	2	Agriculture Extension	3
Livestock- Dairy	3	Landscape Horticulture	2
Farm Mechanization	3	Civics and Development Studies	2
TOTAL	20		20

Belize School of Nursing
(Also known as **Bliss School of Nursing**)
P.O. Box 615
Princess Margaret Drive
Belize City
Tel.: 44062

- **Organization:** Belize School of Nursing, a public, postsecondary institution, offers five programs: a 3-year program leading to the diploma in Professional Nursing, a 1-year program leading to the Practical Nursing Certificate, a 2-year program in Rural Health, and two 1-year programs leading to a Certificate in Midwifery.

- **Admission:** All students must be between 18 and 35 years old. For the Practical Nursing and Rural Health programs, candidates must have completed 2 years of secondary school and hold a primary school certificate. For the Professional Nursing diploma, students must have a secondary school diploma and must have passed three "O level" examinations in English, mathematics, and one of the sciences. After successfully completing the Practical or Professional Nursing programs, students may earn the corresponding Certificate in Practical or Professional Midwifery with an additional year of coursework.

Belize Teachers' College
P.O. Box 579
Princess Margaret Drive
Belize City
Tel.: 34010

- **Organization:** Belize Teachers' College offers a 3-year program in teacher training, leading to a Certificate in Teacher Education. Each year consists of 2 semesters and a summer, followed by 1 semester of student teaching, and then additional coursework, for a total of 3 full years of training. This credential entitles recipients to teach at the primary school level in Belize. The Teachers' College no longer grants a degree for teaching at the secondary school level; students interested in teaching at this level now generally attend the University College of Belize. The most complete description of Belize Teachers' College is found in the original PIER Report on Central America; readers are advised to refer to its comprehensive historical narrative.

Belize Technical College
P.O. Box 366
Freetown Road
Belize City
Tels.: 44024, 44049
Fax: 33577

Established in 1952, Belize Technical College developed from Belize's Technical High School, with assistance from the United Kingdom. Its Associate in Arts and Sciences credential is awarded upon successful completion of 72 credits, which are transcribed in a manner similar to that of a U.S. community college. Associate degree students are not required to sit for "A level" exams in order to graduate, but their coursework is based on an "A level" curriculum. Programs of study are offered in administrative assistant, applied sciences, and non-science tracks. (See Document 2.2)

The grading system follows:

Grade	Description	Quality Point Value
A	Excellent	4.0
B+	Very Good	3.5
B	Good	3.0
C+	Satisfactory	2.5
C	Average	2.0
D+	Below Average	1.5
D	Unsatisfactory	1.0
F	Failure	0.0
Inc.	Incomplete (Requirements outstanding)	
CR	Completed Requirements (non-credit)	
W/P	Withdrawal while Passing	
W/F	Withdrawal while Failing	

Type code
T- repeated initial attempt
R- repeated last attempt

Belmopan Junior College/BJC
Bliss Parade
Belmopan
Belize

Established on August 24, 1992, Belmopan Junior College (BJC) was founded by the University College of Belize. Its purpose was to serve as the first junior college in the country to emphasize a broad-based liberal arts curriculum for the preparation of higher studies in UCB's senior campus in Belize City. BJC was authorized by the Ministry of Education to grant credentials under the University College of Belize Act of 1988. The school is mainly structured to provide students with the first 2 years necessary for entrance to UCB. BJC is located in the nation's capital, and its administration works closely with its Belize City advisory committee at UCB.

- **Organization:** BJC has a library with approximately 3500 volumes, and a computer lab with 18 personal computers. The institution has ten full-time faculty members, offering 2-year associate degrees in Business Administration, Mathematics, English, Business Studies, and Secretarial Studies. In 1993, there were 138 students, nearly all of them studying fulltime. The most popular major to date has been Business Administration.

- **Grading:** BJC's grading system is similar to that of most U.S. colleges and universities. Grades range from "A" (100-95 percent) to "F" (59-0 percent). "D" (60 percent) is the minimum passing grade. Students must have a "C+" (2.5) cumulative grade point average to graduate.

Corozal Junior College
P.O. Box 63
Corozal Town
Corozal

Established in 1986, a sixth form was added to the existing high school to meet the educational needs of the predominantly Spanish-speaking northern sector of Belize. According to the 1980 census Corozal District was more than 75 percent mestizo; but this number can be expected to be much higher today. Other languages spoken are Mayan dialects, Garifuna, and Low German. This linguistic diversity notwithstanding, classes at the college are taught in English. Corozal Junior College is rapidly increasing its standing among Belizean institutions, and surpassed the traditionally top-ranked St. John's College in number of "A level" passes in 1993.

- **Organization:** Corozal offers associate degrees in business, secretarial studies, biology, chemistry, and mathematics. There are approxi-mately 70 students enrolled in the sixth form.

It is important to note that the secondary school affiliated with Corozal Junior College is known as Corozal Community College. Students who progress from the high school to the sixth form (or Junior College) will hold a Community College credential.

- **Grading:**

Letter grade		Point equivalent
A	Superior, Excellent achievement	4.00
A-		3.67
B+		3.33
B	Good, exceeding all requirements	3.00
B-		2.67
C+		2.33
C	Average, satisfactorily meeting all requirements	2.00
C-		1.67
D+		1.33

D	Passing	1.00
D-		0.67
F		0.00
U	Ungraded	0.00
WP	Withdrawal while doing passing work	
WF	Withdrawal while doing failing work	

Muffles College Sixth Form
P.O. Box 64
Orange Walk Town
Belize
Tel: 03-22033

Established in 1989 in response to demands for postsecondary education in Orange Walk Town, when the Ministry of Education requested that Muffles High School expand its curriculum to become a sixth form institution. The Sisters of Mercy, who have administered the school since its inception in 1967, agreed to help meet this need, and Muffles College Sixth Form opened its doors on August 24, 1992. It has 55 full-time students, and graduated its first class of students in June 1994.

- **Organization:** Muffles College offered three programs of study leading to an associate degree as of the 1994-1995 academic year. The options are Business, Secretarial, or General Studies programs.

  The sixth form is housed in one building. Its library is shared with the high school, with a collection of approximately 5,000 volumes. Computer access is limited to projects for school assignments, but the administration has plans to expand computer facilities.

  There are eight instructors teaching at the sixth form level, seven of whom are part-time. They are from the high school faculty and local community, with the exception of the assistant dean, who serves as the fulltime administrator and a faculty member.

- **Academic Year:** The Muffles school year is divided into 2 semesters, from August to May.

- **Admissions:** 1. Applicants must have graduated from high school or its equivalent, and must have obtained a grade of "C" or better in math and English in the final year.

  2. Applicants should rank in the upper half of their graduating class.

  3. They need a satisfactory score in the ACT exam. Applicants also must take the CXC Math and English exams at the general proficiency level.

  4. They must complete an application form and pay an application fee.

  5. They must present two recommendations in support of the application, one from the applicant's

school principal and the other from a secondary school teacher.

- **Grading:**
Muffles Sixth Form uses a letter grading system, defined as follows:

Letter Grade	Quality Point Equivalent	Qualitative Description
A	4.0	Excellent
B+	3.5	Very Good
B	3.0	Good
C+	2.5	Average
C	2.0	Marginal Pass
D	1.0	Unsatisfactory
F	0.0	Failure

- **Academic Requirements:** Muffles College Sixth Form students are required to take a minimum of 18 credit hours each semester of year 1 and a minimum of 17 credit hours each semester of year 2. Each academic program is divided into three categories of courses, namely, the professional core, the support core, and electives. Students take 24 semester hours of support core courses, 12 hours of approved electives, and 34 hours of professional core courses to complete the 70 credit hours required for the associate degree.

- **Professional Core:** Students are required to maintain a professional core grade point average of not less than 2.0, and must have a minimum grade of D in 34 semester hours in this group.

   The professional core courses in business include the following: accounting, economics, business management, marketing, business law, business finance, business ethics, business communication, and computer science. Under this program students may also opt to pursue the economics or accounting "A level" tracks.

   The professional core courses in the secretarial studies program include: accounting, business management, business communications, economics, business data processing, typewriting, computer science, Spanish, note taking, and office management.

- **General Studies:** According to Muffles' program description, the professional core of the General Studies program is designed to help students decide which major they would like to pursue at the university level. Courses include: study skills, speech, computer science, philosophy, science, literature, history, social science, and mathematics.

- **Support Core:** Students are required to maintain at least a "D" in a minimum of 24 semester hours in this core and at least a 2.0 grade point average in the core.
Courses: English, mathematics, and theology.

- **Electives:** Students are required to take a minimum of 12 credit hours of electives. Courses offered are: Introduction to Psychology, Introduction to Sociology, Creative Writing, Making Moral Decisions, Instructional Techniques, Introduction to Computers, History of Western Civilization, Speech, Study Skills, Caribbean Culture, Instructional Techniques, Introduction to Politics, Educational Psychology, and Introduction to Philosophy.

St. John's College Sixth Form
P.O. Box 548
Belize City
Tel. 33732
Fax. 32752

Established in 1887, St. John's College was granted the status of an advanced level ("A level") school by Cambridge University soon thereafter. The sixth form program of postsecondary education was inaugurated in 1952. During the 1960s, the sixth form broadened its programs to meet the "requirements of the associate degree awarded by junior and community colleges in the United States... This enabled graduates of St. John's College Sixth Form to enter Commonwealth institutions which require Cambridge University "A level" certificates, and also U.S. universities, as transfer students, into the third year of the Bachelor's Degree programs." (From SJC's 1993 *Advanced Studies Bulletin*).

   On August 9, 1966, the Government of Belize approved the associate degree. At the same time, St. John's College joined the American Association of Community and Junior Colleges. It is also a member of the U.S. Association of Jesuit Colleges and Universities.

- **Organization:** The St. John's *Bulletin* distinguishes between the "A level" and associate degree programs: "Students opting for the narrower and more specialized Cambridge University "A level" syllabuses will also qualify for the award of an associate degree. Students opting for the broader programs of the associate degree may not have specialized enough to sit the Cambridge "A level" examinations. Despite this distinction, it is important to note that all successful students, regardless of their "A level" results, graduate with an associate degree. (See Document 2.3)

   Traditionally considered the top-ranked postsecondary institution in Belize, St. John's College currently offers 2-year associate degrees in science, arts, arts and science, business, general studies, and secretarial science. In 1994, there were 510 sixth form students, 481 of whom study fulltime, 17 credit hours per semester. Located on a 40-acre campus in Belize City, the College consists of 17 classrooms, and biology, chemistry, physics, computer, audiovisual, and typing laboratories. It also has a field house with basketball courts and playing fields.

The institution's most popular majors are business and general studies. The faculty consists of 34 fulltime and 8 part-time professors. The majority of the faculty possess a bachelor's degree (32), while others hold either master's or doctoral degrees. There are also two faculty members who have only completed the sixth form level. Between 1988 and 1993, the College awarded 823 associate degrees.

- **Grading:** St. John's is consistent with other Belizean (and most U.S.) institutions: grades range from "A" to "F." "D" is the lowest minimum passing grade, and students must have at least a "C" average to graduate.

Stann Creek Ecumenical College
P.O. Box 84
Dangriga, Belize
Tel: 05-22654, 05-22114

Established in 1986, Stann Creek Ecumenical College is a sixth form institution with an emphasis on business and the natural and physical sciences.

- **Admission:** Either a CXC (grades I or II) or GCE pass in general level English language. In addition, science students must pass either CXC general level mathematics (grades I or II) or GCE Mathematics. Every science student and every history major must have passed either General level (grades I or II) or GCE in their desired major courses.

Students must also present ACT scores and Ecumenical College Placement Test (E.C.P.T.) scores to be considered for admission. Areas examined in the E.C.P.T. are English language, chemistry, physics, biology and mathematics.

Students can currently earn an associate degree in one of the following four areas: science, arts, arts and science, and business. Associate degrees are 72-hour programs.

Science: concentrations are offered in biology, chemistry, and mathematics.

Arts: concentrations are offered in economics and history.

Arts/Science: concentrations are offered in history and biology; economics and biology; economics and chemistry; economics and math; economics, physics, and math.

Business: concentration offered in business.

- **Grading:** Grading system ranges from "A" to "F;" with students remaining in good academic standing as long as they maintain at least a 2.0 grade point average.

Toledo Community College
Punta Gorda Town
Toledo District

The secondary-level Toledo Community College is developing a sixth form program that will serve students in the southernmost point of Belize, in Punta Gorda. The program is being designed with the assistance of the University College of Belize.

University College of Belize/UCB
P.O. Box 990
West Landivar
Belize City
Tel: 30255

Established in 1986, the University College of Belize/UCB, was established with the administrative and academic assistance of Ferris State University of Michigan. In its first year, it enrolled 105 students in business administration, pharmacy, medical lab technology, and English as a Second Language. Students enrolled held an associate degree from one of the sixth forms in Belize. Two years later, UCB graduated its first four students in Business Administration, granting joint UCB-Ferris State bachelor's degrees, under the Michigan institution's authority.

The university college was established formally in 1988, when the Belizean government passed the University College of Belize Act, recognizing its credential-granting status. The University College of Belize is the only accredited bachelor's degree-granting institution in Belize.

The following year, in 1989, UCB dedicated its first building, moving away from its temporary quarters at Belize Teacher's College, and in 1990 the university ended its contractual agreement with Ferris State University.

In 1993, UCB had 451 students, approximately one-half of whom were studying full-time (at least 12 credit hours per semester.) The institution has 44 professors, 27 full-time and 17 part-time. Nine faculty members possess doctoral degrees, 18 master's degrees, and the remaining 14 have either bachelor's or sixth form degrees.

- **Organization:** UCB's campus is located in Belize City. It consists of one modern three-story building, housing seven classrooms, two science laboratories, a library, and administrative offices. The library collection contains over 10,000 circulating volumes and approx-imately 2,000 reference volumes. It also has five computers available for student use. UCB also has a science building containing two additional science laboratories, classrooms, and office space. The university has recently leased an island, Middle Long Caye, for the construction of a marine research facility. In 1992, the Government of Belize author-ized the university to open a campus in the nation's capital, Belmopan, offering associate degree pro-grams to prepare students for their final 2 years of study at UCB.

- **Admission:** Following are UCB's general admis-sion requirements:

<u>Bachelor's Degree Programs</u>
1. Completion of an associate degree program or equivalent, from a government-recognized postsec-ondary level institution, with a minimum grade point average (GPA) of 2.5 (out of 4.0).
2. Meet any other specified requirement of a given program.
3. Take and pass a UCB matriculation examination.
4. Complete an application form and pay an applica-tion fee.
5. Present two recommendations in support of the application.
The academic programs also have specific admis-sions requirements for candidates. For example, applicants for the program in chemistry education must have majored in chemistry at the junior college level and have a GPA of 2.5 in chemistry in previous coursework. Candidates for the biology education program must have received a grade of "C" or better in chemistry in their last year of high school or have scored a grade of I or II in the Caribbean Examinations Council's General Profic-iency Chemistry examination, or equivalent in an-other external examination.

<u>Associate Degree in Applied Sciences Programs</u>
Students are generally required to fulfill the same re-quirements outlined above, except that rather than completing a 2-year postsecondary degree, they must satisfy one of the following:
A. Passes in four GCE or CXC subjects (CXC grades I and II at the general proficiency level are considered passes.) Grade I at the basic proficiency

level and may be considered on a case by case basis one of the four required passes; or
B. A high school diploma or equivalent and a tran-script showing a "C" (70 percent) average or higher and a score of "C" or higher in biology, chemistry, English, and mathematics in the last year of high school; or
c. A score in the American College Test deemed ade-quate by UCB.

<u>Certificate or Diploma Programs</u>
Students are required to fulfill the same requirements outlined for the bachelor's degree, except that rather than having to have completed a 2-year postsec-ondary degree, they must possess a high school diploma or its equivalent. For the English as a Second Language (ESL) program, students must be at least 17 years old by the end of the first semester of attendance.

- **Grading:** UCB's grading system is similar to that of U.S. colleges and universities. Grades range from "A" (100-95 percent) to "F" (59-0 percent). Letter grades are "A," "A-," "B+," "B," "C+," "C," "D+," "D," and "F." "D" (64-60 percent) is the minimum passing grade. Students in the bachelor's degree and Allied Health programs must maintain at least a 2.5 cumulative grade point average to remain in good academic standing. In the Para Legal and English as a Second Language programs, the minimum cumulative GPA to remain in good academic standing is 2.0. Students who do not meet these standards are placed on academic probation and may be required to withdraw from UCB.

- **Organization:** UCB's bachelor's degree programs provide the third and fourth years of university studies. Nearly all students enter as transfer students from Belizean postsecondary institutions and each program has different requirements for total numbers of credits needed to earn a UCB degree.

  Transcripts from junior college, sixth form, and other postsecondary schools are reviewed for processing transfer credits. Each department at UCB may accept credit for courses completed at recognized institutions, which the different departments may deem equivalent to those required by the UCB degree program. Only courses in which a student has received a grade of "C" or better may be accepted. Each department determines the maximum number of transfer credits a student may receive, ranging from 58 to 62 semester credit hours.

- **Course Requirements:** All students, regardless of their academic area, must complete general core requirements consisting of 12 semester hours of humanities, 9 hours of mathematics and natural sciences, and 9 hours of social sciences. Additionally they are required to take 1 semester hour of study skills. In all, the program requires each student to take 44 semester hours for the general core, 31 of which are described above.

The remaining requirements for the bachelor's degree are divided between Junior and Senior College Level Courses. Most programs require between 130 and 134 total credits for graduation. A typical program consists of the 44 hours of general core studies (which are taken at the Junior College Level), 15-20 semester hours of Junior College Level classes, and 67-77 hours of UCB Level classes.

• **Credentials Awarded:** The English as a Second Language Certificate program is a 1-year, full-time intensive English program, designed to help native Spanish-speaking students prepare for the Test of English as a Foreign Language (TOEFL) examination for admission to Junior College. To pass the course, students must take an oral and written examination, complete 26.5 semester credit hours of courses, complete a community service exercise, and maintain a cumulative GPA of at least 2.0.

The Certificate in Para Legal Studies program is a 2-year, part-time program, created to teach the general principles of English and Belizean law. It covers 12 topics, and requires a course in Belizean History. Ninteen credit hours are required by the program, and students must maintain a minimum cumulative GPA of 2.0.

UCB offers four Associate Degrees in Applied Sciences, with majors in Medical Laboratory Technology, Environmental Health, Court Reporting, and Pharmacy. These full-time programs require approximately 80 to 100 credit hours of coursework.

Bachelor's degrees are offered in Education and Business Adfministration. In the Education program, students may opt for one of the following concentrations: biology, business education, chemistry, English, or mathematics.

Glossary

"A level." General Certificate of Education Advanced Level examination

CXC. Caribbean Examinations Council

CGLI. City and Guilds of London Institute examinations

Community College. Secondary-level school

GCE. General Certificate of Education

"O level." General Certificate of Education Ordinary Level examination

Para Legal. Paralegal

Sixth Form. 2-year postsecondary programs

COROZAL JUNIOR COLLEGE
P.O. Box 63
Corozal Town

OFFICE OF THE DEAN

STUDENT NAME: _____ _____ FIRST _____
MIDDLE

BIRTH DATE: _____ LAST 20TH SEPTEMBER, 1974

ADDRESS: _____ _____ COROZAL DISTRICT, BELIZE CENTRAL AMERICA.

PARENT/GUARDIAN _____ _____ PHONE: 04 - 30188

Period Ending	Course Number	Course Title	Credit	Grade	Quality Points
SEPT. 91	131	Inter. Accounting I	3	B+	9.99
	101	Bus. Management I	3	B-	8.01
	203-3	Desktop Publishing	3	B+	9.99
JAN. 91	105	Prin. of Economics I	3	A-	11.01
	153	English in bus. I	3	B+	9.99
	110	Business Math I	3	B+	9.99
	175	Introduction to Psychology I	3	A	12.00
		Q. P. A. = 3.38			
JAN. 92	132	Intermediate Accounting II	3	B	9.00
	102	Business Management II	3	B	9.00
	106	Principles of Economics I	3	B+	9.99
JUNE 92	154	English in Business I	3	B+	9.99
	111	Business Math I	3	B-	8.01
	176	Introduction to Psy. I	3	B+	9.99
		Q.P.A. = 3.11			

MAJOR: BUSINESS STUDIES

REGISTRATION DATE: SEPTEMBER 1991

ADMITTED FROM: COROZAL COMMUNITY COLLEGE

GRADUATED: 6TH JUNE, 1993.

AWARD CONFERRED: ASSOCIATE DEGREE IN BUSINESS STUDIES

WITHDREW: _____

ACT/SAT SCORES: VERBAL | MATH | SCIENCE | SOCIAL STUDIES

CXC PASSES: _____

GCE 'A' PASSES: _____

Period Ending	Course Number	Course Title	Credit	Grade	Quality Points
SEPT. 92	AC 233	Advanced Accounting I	3	B+	9.99
	BU 221	Business Law I	3	B	9.00
	BU 223	Business Finance I	3	A-	11.01
JAN. 93	EN 255	English in Bus. II	3	B+	9.99
	BU 213	Principles of Marketing I	3	B+	9.99
	MT 225	Business Stat. I	3	B+	9.99
		Q.P.A. = 3.33			
JAN. 93	AC 234	Advanced Acctg. II	3	A-	11.01
	BU 222	Business Law II	3	A-	11.01
	BU 224	Business Finance II	3	B	9.00
JUNE 93	EN 256	English in Business II	3	A-	11.01
	BU 214	Prin. of Marketg. II	3	C+	6.99
	MT 226	Bus. Statistics II	3	B	9.00
		Q.P.A. = 3.22			

Cumulative Q.P.A. = 3.27

GRADING SYSTEM:

	Grade	Quality Points
A	Excellent	4.0
B+	Very Good	3.5
B	Good	3.0
C+	Above Average	2.5
C	Average	2.0
D+	Below Average	1.5
D	Minimal Pass	1.0
F	Failure	0.0
WP	Withdrawal Passing	
WF	Withdrawal Failing	
I	Incomplete	

This is a true and correct copy of the official record of the above named student when signed and sealed it is an official transcript.

Jose Mai

ᵞ Dean, Corozal Junior College

Date: 15th September, 1993.

Document 2.1 A postsecondary transcript from Corozal Junior College
(NOTE: Corozal *Community* College is a secondary institution)

BELIZE TECHNICAL COLLEGE
FREETOWN ROAD, BELIZE CITY
BELIZE, C.A.

Phone: 44024/44049
Fax: 33577

TRANSCRIPT OF GRADES

STUDENT NAME: ....

DATE OF BIRTH: .... 5th MAY 1973 ....

PROGRAMME: .... SIXTH FORM (UNIVERSITY PREPARATION) NON-SCIENCE ....

DATE OF ENTRY: 19th AUGUST 1991 .... DATE OF GRADUATION: 13th JUNE 1993

NUMBER	TITLE	Type	Grade	Course Credit	Credit Earned	Quality Points
	FIRST SEMESTER					
Econ 101	Micro I		B+	6	6	21.00
Acc 101	Accounting		A	6	6	24.00
BL 101	Business Law		B+	3	3	10.50
GS 101	English Composition I		B	3	3	9.00
	SEMESTER TOTAL		3.58	18	18	64.50
	SECOND SEMESTER					
Econ 102	Micro II		B	6	6	18.00
Acc 102	Accounting		A	6	6	24.00
BL 102	Business Law		A	3	3	12.00
GS 102	English Composition II		B	3	3	9.00
	SEMESTER TOTAL		3.50	18	18	63.00
	THIRD SEMESTER					
Econ 201	Macro I		B+	6	6	21.00
Acc 201	Accounting		A	6	6	24.00
BH 201	Belizean History		A	3	3	12.00
GS 201	English & Composition		B+	3	3	10.50
	SEMESTER TOTAL		3.75	18	18	67.50
	FOURTH SEMESTER					
BH 202	Belizean History		B+	3	3	10.50
Math207	Statistics		B	3	3	9.00
Econ 202	Macro II		A	6	6	24.00
GS 202	English & Composition		B+	3	3	10.50
Acc 202	Managerial Accounting		A	6	6	24.00
	SEMESTER TOTAL		3.71	21	21	78.00
	CUMULATIVE		3.64	75	75	273.00

END OF TRANSCRIPT XXXXXXXXXXXXXXXXXXXXXXXXXXXXXXXXXXXXXXXX

Document 2.2 A "non-science" transcript from Belize Technical College

Permanent record

ST. JOHN'S COLLEGE
(Sixth Form)
BELIZE CITY, BELIZE (British Honduras)
CENTRAL AMERICA

Office of the Dean

Name	[illegible]	Date of birth	July 11, 1972
Address	[illegible], Belize City, Belize	Place of birth	Belize City, Belize
Parent or Guardian	[illegible]	Date entered	August 22,1988
Address	[illegible], Belize City, Belize	Graduated	May 27, 1990
High School work at	Pallotti High School	Withdrew	
Admitted from	" " "	Degree	Associate Arts

Course	No.	Descriptive Title	GRADE	CREDIT HOURS	CREDIT POINTS	Course	No.	Descriptive Title	GRADE	CREDIT HOURS	CREDIT POINTS
First year/Sem. I						Second year/Sem. I					
En	135	Shakespeare	B	5	15.0	En	245	Victorian Lit.	B	5	15.0
Hist	143	European History	B	5	15.0	Hist	245	English History	B	5	15.0
En	103	Grammar & Comp.	A	3	12.0	En	243	Adv. Engl. Comp	B+	3	10.5
Spe	202	Basic Skills of Speech	A	2	8.0	Psy	194	Personality Dev.	A	3	12.0
						Ec	109	Development Ec.	A	3	12.0
First year/Sem. II						Second year/Sem. II					
En	136	Chaucer & Other Major Authors	B	5	15.0	En	246	Victorian Lit.II	B	5	15.0
Hist	144	European History	B	5	15.0	Hist	246	English History	B	5	15.0
En	104	Grammar & Comp.	A	3	12.0	En	244	Adv. Eng. Comp.	B	3	9.0
Psy	193	Intro./Psychology	C+	3	7.5	Cps	105	Appl. Software	A	2	8.0
Th	119	Moral Decisions	B+	3	10.5	Th	127	Intro. to Christianity	A	3	12.0
							Total Average: 3.3				

Sample Document

*transfer credits accepted from

A	-Excellent	4.0 credit pts.	D	-Pass	1.0 credit pts.
B+	-Very Good	3.5 credit pts.	F	-Failure	0 credit pts.
B	-Good	3.0 credit pts.	I	-Incomplete, passing but must meet requirements	
C+	-Satisfactory	2.5 credit pts.	Wf	-Withdrew Failing	
C	-Satisfactory	2.0 credit pts.	Wp	-Withdrew Passing	

ONE CREDIT HOUR .... one 50 min. class or two 50 min. lab. periods.

SCHOOL YEAR .... 32 weeks.

Results of tests, I.Q., achievement, etc.

St. John's Junior College P. O. Box 548 Belize City Belize, C. A.

S. Mercy Cervantes, RSM

Requirements for Associate Degree .... minimum of 56 credit hours and 2.00 point average on work attempted.

Total credit hrs. gained by candidate. 71

C.X.C. + G.C.E. results . . . . O and A level

G.C.E. "A" LEVEL: English (D) History (O), General Paper ( ).

Document 2.3 This student received the Associate Degree and took the "A Level" examinations

Chapter 3
The Educational System of Costa Rica

The Country

A peaceful, democratic nation, Costa Rica prides itself on being the only Central American country without an army. Although often literally surrounded by neighboring strife, it was largely spared from its neighbors' military disputes of the 1980s, and has enjoyed relative economic prosperity with an accompanying peace and tranquility. The early 1990s brought a degree of economic hardship to Costa Rica, with some social unrest, but overall conditions remain stable and conducive to the maintenance of a strong public education system.

The people

Unlike its neighbors on the Central American isthmus, Costa Rica has never had a large indigenous population. Its current inhabitants look very much like their European ancestors, who crossed the ocean as immigrants from Spain, Germany, the Netherlands, Switzerland, and Great Britain to settle in Costa Rica. The nation's indigenous population today numbers approximately 25,000. On the Atlantic Coast, the population is more Afro-Caribbean and English-speaking than in the nation's interior.

Postsecondary Education

The first Costa Rican institution of higher education, the *Universidad de Santo Tomás*, was founded on May 3, 1843 by then head of state Juan Mora Fernández. It consisted of faculties of humanities, sciences, math and physics, and theology and ecclesiastic sciences. Like its contemporary successors, the university awarded *bachiller* and *licenciado* credentials. It was abolished in 1888 (*Prensa Libre,* April 19, 1994, p. 5C).

This century's system of higher education began with the foundation of the *Universidad de Costa Rica/ UCR* in 1940. *UCR* assumed responsibility for all higher education and remained the only postsecondary institution until 1968, when the *Escuela Normal Nacional Superior* (National Higher Normal School) was established. In 1971, the *Instituto Tecnológico de Costa*

Official name: Republic of Costa Rica

Area: 51,032 square kilometers/19,652 square miles (slightly smaller than West Virginia)

Capital: San José

Population: 3 million

Annual growth rate: 2.5 percent

Noun and adjective: Costa Rican(s)

Ethnic groups: European (including some Mestizos) 96%; Black 3%; indigenous 1%.

Religions: Roman Catholic

Languages: Spanish, with Jamaican dialect of English spoken around Puerto Limón

Education: Years compulsory-6; Attendance - nearly 100%; Literacy-93%.

(Source: U.S. State Department *Background Notes*)

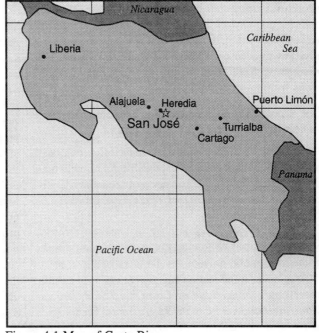

Figure 4.1 Map of Costa Rica

Rica/ITCR (Technological Institute of Costa Rica) was founded, to be followed two years later by the *Universidad Nacional/UNA* (National University), for which the National Higher Normal School was the original institution. The most recent state university, the *Universidad Estatal a Distancia/UNED* (State University at a Distance) began operation in 1977. The number of public Costa Rican universities has remained constant at four.

In 1976, the first private university, (*Universidad Autónoma de Centro América/UACA*) opened its doors. Since 1980, the number of private universities has increased dramatically, until there are approximately 15 authorized to grant credentials in Costa Rica Several explanations have been offered for this "boom" in private institutions. The most probable reason is capacity: the four state universities are full, and simply lack the ability to accommodate the increasing demand for higher education. Their admission standards have become tougher, and they are rejecting increasing numbers of candidates. Students are turning to private universities as an alternative. Costa Rica may soon face a situation analogous to El Salvador, in which minimum academic, programmatic, and professional standards must be reexamined to deal with the relatively unregulated private institutions.

Other categories of institutions in Costa Rica include branches of foreign universities and the unique *Universidad para la Paz*, established and run by the United Nations (see institutional description below). There are also numerous "parauniversities" (*parauniversidades*), which are similar to U.S. community colleges. A few of these institutions are mentioned at the end of this chapter. Several parauniversities have developed cooperative agreements with the new private universities, in which the universities accept transfer credit for coursework completed at these non-university institutions. Although *parauniversidades* must be approved by the *Consejo Superior de Educación*, the public universities have traditionally not accepted transfer credits from these institutions.

The *Consejo Superior de Educación* and *Consejo Nacional de Rectores*

The *Consejo Superior de Educación* (Higher Council for Education) is the body responsible for establishing educational policy at the primary and secondary levels, and for the *parauniversidades* (parauniversities) at the postsecondary level.

The *Consejo Nacional de Rectores/CONARE* (National Council of Rectors) is the coordinating body for the four public universities. Its membership consists of the minister of education and the rectors of the public universities: *Universidad de Costa Rica/UCR, Universidad Nacional Autónoma/UNA, Instituto Tecnológico de Costa Rica/ITCR*, and *Universidad Estatal a Distancia/UNED*.

The public universities require that students take a program of general studies (*estudios generales*). According to *CONARE*, students who hold a *bachiller universitario* credential from a public institution do not necessarily have to pass the general studies requirement to progress to a more advanced level of study at a state university. However, graduates of private universities must certify that they have passed this core requirement or its equivalent in order to enroll in an advanced degree program at a public institution.

The *Consejo Nacional de Educación Superior de Universidades Privadas/CONESUP* (National Council of Higher Education for Private Universities) is the supervising authority for the Costa Rican private universities.

The membership of *CONESUP* consists of the minister of education and one representative of each of the following: *CONARE*, Ministry of National Planning, the private universities, and the Federation of Professional Societies of Costa Rica.

Credentials, Diplomas, and Certificates

Three levels are used to categorize academic courses of study: *pregrado, grado, postgrado* (preuniversity credential, first university credential, and graduate credential). *Pregrado* includes those courses of study of short duration, *carreras cortas* or intermediate credentials, for which diplomas may be given, but which do not earn the holders the distinction of being professionals. (Note: *postgrado* may be spelled *posgrado* on some documents.)

Degrees in Costa Rica are based on the completion of a defined amount of course work and other requirements. Each course is given a credit rating. Each credit requires 15 hours of classroom work or 45 hours of laboratory or practical training.

The following are the university-level credentials awarded in Costa Rica. This information was originally reported in the 1987 PIER Report on Central America.

Diplomado (Diplomate), *Asociado* (Associate), or *Técnico Superior* (Higher Level Technician): A *pregrado* diploma course that requires a minimum of 60 units and a maximum of 90 units. Among the two types, terminal and non-terminal, most of these programs are considered terminal except for those offered at the *Instituto Tecnólogico de Costa Rica*, where the *diplomado* is earned en route to the *bachiller universitario*. All or part of the units completed in a non-terminal program may be credited to a degree program. The minimum time to complete a diploma program is 4 semesters (2.66 at ITCR because it operates on 18-week semesters). The *diplomado* is occasionally referred to as a *diplomado universitario*, and the *asociado* credential is awarded at some institutions upon successful completion of the 2-year *técnico superior* program.

Profesor (Teacher): A 3-year *pregrado* program which trains preschool and primary school teachers.

Bachiller Universitario/BU (university-level Bachiller): The first university (*grado*) credential awarded in Costa Rica. Holders of the BU may enter directly into a master's degree program in the same field, if it exists, and they are eligible to teach at the university level. Note: Although the *bachiller universitario* is frequently referred to as a *bachiller*, it should not be confused with the secondary-level *bachiller* or *bachillerato*, the common Central American name for the secondary credential.

Licenciatura, Licenciado (Licentiate): T h e *licenciado* program, a *grado* credential, is a minimum of 30 and a maximum of 36 units beyond the *bachiller* program. It is generally awarded as the first credential in certain fields such as medicine, law, and dentistry.

Especialización/Especialidad Profesional (Profes-sional Specialization/Specialty): *Postgrado* degree offered in medicine and law, these are programs of a professional specialization which requires a recognized university credential for entrance and are considered post-graduate studies.

Maestría (Master's): *Postgrado* level. Represents a minimum of 60 units, or 4 semesters, of study beyond the *bachiller universitario*. A thesis is required for graduation, and research activities are stressed.

Doctorado, Doctor (Doctorate): *Postgrado* degree, requiring a minimum of 100 units and maximum of 120 beyond the *bachiller universitario*. A thesis is required. Advanced standing may be granted for units previously completed in a *maestría* or *licenciado* program.

In Costa Rica a distinction is made between the credential and the title received in a given specialization. For example, a successful candidate in Industrial Production Engineering earns the title "*Ingeniero en Producción Industrial*" and the credential "*Bachiller* or *Bachillerato Universitario*." For the purposes of this report, the credential, not the title, is listed.

Institutional Profiles

Instituto Tecnólogico de Costa Rica/ITCR (Technological Institute of Costa Rica)
Department of Admissions and Registration
Apartado Postal 159-7050
Cartago
Tel: (506) 551-5333 Ext. 2308-2255
Fax: (506) 551-5348

Established and authorized to award credentials: June 10, 1971. The *ITCR* is a university-level state institution. It was founded to advance the scientific, and technological development of Costa Rica. In addition to its main campus in Cartago, *ITCR* has a regional center in San Carlos (*Alajuela* province), and an academic center in the capital city, San José.

- **Admissions:** Applicants for postsecondary programs must hold a secondary-level *bachiller* or its equivalent and must pass an entrance examination. Candidates for graduate level (*maestría*) programs are required to hold at least a *bachiller universitario*.

- **Credentials Awarded:** The credentials listed below are academic degrees (*grados académicos*), not titles (*títulos*) awarded. This is an important distinction, because each specialization has both a credential and a title associated with it. For example, a student who completes a program in Business Administration (*Administración de Empresas*), earns the title "*Administrador de Empresas*" (Business Administrator). He or she earns the credential *bachiller universitario* or *licenciado*, depending upon the program taken.

   At the main campus in Cartago, the following programs are offered:

Programs offered	Credential/years
Administrative Agricultural Engineering with Emphasis in:	
Agricultural Business	*bachiller universitario* 4, *licenciado* 5
Agroindustrial Business	*bachiller universitario* 4, *icenciado* 5
Business Administration with emphasis in:	*bachiller universitario* 4 (day); 5 (evening)
Human Resources	*licenciado* 5, *maestría* 6
Agronomist	*bachiller universitario, licenciado* 5
Agricultural Engineer	*bachiller universitario* 4, *licenciado* 5
Metallurgy Engineer	*bachiller universitario* 4
Industrial Maintenance Engineer	*bachiller universitario* 4, *licenciado* 5
Industrial Production Engineer	*bachiller universitario* 4, *licenciado* 5
Occupational Security and Hygiene	*asociado* 2, *bachiller universitario* 4

At the San Carlos campus, the following programs are offered:

Programs offered	Credential/years
Business Administration	*bachiller universitario* 4
Agronomist	*bachiller universitario* 4, *licenciado* 5
Computer Engineer	*bachiller universitario* 4

At the San José Academic Center, the following programs are offered:

Programs offered	Credential/years
Business Administration	*bachiller universitario* 4, *licenciado* 5, *maestría* 6
Production Supervision	*asociado* 2
Architectural and Engr. Drawing	*asociado* 2

Universidad Adventista de Centro América/UNADECA
(Adventist University of Central America)
Apartado 138
Carretera Itiquis
Alajuela
Tel.: 41-5622

Established and authorized to grant credentials: July 22, 1987

Programs offered	Credential
Business Administration with emphasis in:	
Accounting	*bachiller universitario*
Management	*bachiller universitario*
Education with emphasis in:	
Natural Sciences	*bachiller universitario*
Computation	*bachiller universitario*
Religious Education	*bachiller universitario*
Spanish	*bachiller universitario*
Social Studies	*bachiller universitario*
I y II Ciclo Educación General Básica	
English	
Mathematics	
Music	
Pre-School	
Secretary	
Theology	*bachiller universitario*
Professional Executive Secretary	*bachiller universitario*
Bilingual Professional Executive Secretary	*bachiller universitario*
Nursing	*bachiller universitario, licenciado*

Universidad Anselmo Llorente y La Fuente (Anselmo Llorente y La Fuente University)

Established and authorized by *CONESUP* to grant credentialss: May 27, 1993

Programs offered	Credential
Philosophy and Humanities	*bachiller universitario*
Theology	*bachiller universitario, licenciado*
Education with emphasis in	*licenciado*

Programs offered	Credential
Religious education for III Cycle (Secondary School) and Diversified Education	*bachiller universitario, licenciado*
Education for I and II Cycles (Elementary School) of Basic General Education	*bachiller universitario, licenciado*

Universidad Autónoma de Centro América/ UACA (**Autonomous University of Central America**)
Apartado 7637
Calle 33, Av. 8
1000 San José
Tel.: 234-0701
Fax.: 224-0391

Established and authorized by *CONESUP* to grant credentials: December 23, 1975

• **Academic Year:** The academic year runs from January to December and is divided into 3 trimesters of 15 weeks each. The exception is the medical school, which operates on 2 semesters of 22 weeks each. The *UACA* consists of affiliated colleges, each of which is autonomous administratively and financially, but subject to academic standards determined by the central administration. As of August 1993, the following "Colleges" (*colegios*) and academic programs at the *UACA* were recognized by the Ministry of Education.

College or School	Program	Credential
Colegium Academicum Barrio Fco. Peralta 100 mts. sur del Colegio SEK San José Tel.: 234-0701 Fax: 224-0391	Administration Law Economics International Relations Computer Systems	*bachiller universitario* *bachiller universitario, licendiado* *bachiller universitario* *bachiller universitario, licendiado* *bachiller universitario*
Colegio Andrés Bello Barrio La California frente a Pizza Hut, casa 2585 San José Tel.: 223-9282 Fax: 233-0598	Nursing Psychology International Relations Public Relations Education with emphasis in preschool education Tourism	*bachiller universitario, licendiado* *bachiller universitario, licenciado* *bachiller universitario, licendiado* *bachiller universitario, licendiado* *bachiller universitario* *bachiller universitario, licendiado*
Colegio de Artes Plásticas Barrio Fco. Peralta 100 mts. sur del Colegio SEK San José Tel.: 234-0701 Fax: 224-0391	Fine Arts Advertising Design Music	*bachiller universitario* *bachiller universitario* *bachiller universitario*
Escuela Autónoma de Ciencias Médicas de Centro América (Autonomous School of Medical Sciences of Central America) Barrio Fco. Peralta 100 mts. sur del Colegio SEK Tel.: 234-0701 Fax: 224-0391	*Administration of Health* Centers and Services Anatomy-Morphology Health Sciences History of Medicine Medicine Labor Medicine Medicine Medicine	*licenciado, maestría* *maestría* *bachiller universitario* *maestría* *licenciado* *maestría* *licenciado** *doctor***

* Awarded after eight semesters of study
** Awarded after 5 years of study plus internship

College or School *(continued-)*	Program	Credential
Colegium Fidelitas Barrio Escalante 50 norte y 75 oeste del Centro Cultural Norteamericano Tel.: 253-0262 Fax: 253-9576	Administration Administration with emphasis in Finance and Banking Administration with emphasis in Marketing Business Administration Pre-School Education Accounting Public Accounting Industrial Engineering	*bachiller universitario* *licenciado* *licenciado* *licenciado* *bachiller universitario* *bachiller universitario* *licenciado* *bachiller universitario licenciado*
Colleguim Latinum	Business Administration Business Administration Education Sciences Pre-School Education Sciences Elementary (I and II Cycles) Education Sciences Elementary (I and II Cycles) Education Sciences Economics Economics Philosophy History Advertising Advertising International Relations International Relations Public Relations Public Relations	*bachiller universitario* *licenciado* *maestría* *bachiller universitario* *bachiller universitario* *licenciado* *bachiller universitario* *licenciado* *maestría* *maestría* *bachiller universitario* *licenciado* *bachiller universitario* *licenciado* *bachiller universitario* *licenciado*

Colegio Leonardo Da Vinci
 Paseo Colón
 diagonal Pollos Kentucky
 San José
 Tel.: 221-5948
	Administration
	 Business Administration
	 Industrial Administration
	 Basic Sciences of
	     Civil Engineering
	     Industrial Engineering
	     Public Relations
		bachiller universitario
		 licenciado
		 licenciado, maestría
		
		 bachiller universitario, licenciado
		 bachiller universitario
		 bachiller universitario licenciado

Escuela Libre de Derecho Barrio Fco. Peralta 100 mts. sur del Colegio SEK San José Tel.: 234-0701 Fax: 224-0391	Law	*bachiller universitario* *licenciado, doctorado*
Colegio Monterey Barrio Escalante calle 25, Av. 9 San José Tels.: 222-9863, 223-5615 Fax: 222-3062	Administration Administration with emphasis on Finance and Banking Business Administration Human Resource Administration Accounting Public Accounting Psychology Law Computer Systems	*bachiller universitario* *licenciado* *licenciado* *bachiller universitario, licenciado* *bachiller universitario* *licenciado* *bachiller universitario, licenciado* *bachiller universitario, licenciado* *bachiller universitario*

College or School *(continued-)*	Program	Credential

Colegio San Judas Tadeo
Calle 30 sur, Avs. 6 y 10
Barrio San Bosco
San José
Tel.: 221-5948
Fax: 233-3973
	Education
	  with emphasis in I and II Cycle
	  Pre-school Education
	  Journalism
		
		bachiller universitario
		bachiller universitario
		bachiller universitario

Colegio Santo Tomás de Aquino Frente Museo Nacional San José Tels.: 223-2767, 257-1565 Fax: 257-0104	Administration Administration with emphasis in Finance and Banking Business Administration Law Computer Systems	*bachiller universitario* *licenciado* *licenciado* *bachiller universitario, licenciado* *bachiller universitario*

Colegio Stvivm Generale Costariccense	Administration
	Business Administration
	Architecture
	Basic Sciences of
	  Civil Engineering
	  Accounting
	  Public Accounting
	Law
	Economics
	Philology
	Spanish Philology
	Philosophy
	Geography
	History
	Civil Engineering
	Computer Engineering
	Electrical Engineering
	Music
	Journalism
	Computer Systems
		bachiller universitario
		licenciado
		bachiller universitario, licenciado
		
		bachiller universitario
		bachiller universitario
		licenciado
		bachiller universitario, licenciado
		bachiller universitario, licenciado
		bachiller universitario
		licenciado
		bachiller universitario, licenciado
		bachiller universitario
		bachiller universitario
		licenciado
		licenciado
		bachiller universitario
		bachiller universitario, licenciado
		licenciado
		bachiller universitario

Colegio Veritas	Administration Business Administration Architecture Organizational and Informational Sciences Industrial Design Advertising Design Electronic Engineering	*bachiller universitario* *licenciado* *bachiller universitario, licenciado* *bachiller universitario* *bachiller universitario* *bachiller universitario* *bachiller universitario, licenciado*

Universidad Braulio Carillo
(Braulio Carillo University)

Established and authorized by *CONESUP* to grant credentials: February 3, 1994. No further information is available at this time.

Universidad Central Costarricense/UCC (Central Costa Rican University)
De la Iglesia Sta. Teresita
200 Norte y 200 Este
Barrio Escalante
San José
Tel.: 224-0551

Established and authorized by *CONESUP* to grant credentials: March 27, 1990

Programs offered	Credential
Business Administration	*bachiller universitario, licenciado*
Computer Sciences	*bachiller universitario*
Education sciences with emphasis on First and Second Cycle (Elem. Ed.)	*bachiller universitario*

Universidad de Costa Rica/UCR
(University of Costa Rica)
Main Campus:
Ciudad Universitaria "Rodrigo Facio"
San Pedro de Montes de Oca
San José
Tel: 253-5323, 253-3253
Fax: 234-0452

Established in 1940. Branch campuses in: San Ramón, Tacares, Atlántico, Liberia, Santa Cruz, Limón, Puntarenas.

- **Academic calendar:** First cycle runs from February to June; second cycle, August to December; third cycle, January to February.

- **Admission:** secondary school graduation and passage of admissions examination (*prueba de aptitud académica*).

- **Grading:** scale 0 to 10; minimum passing is 7.

- **Enrollment:** 30,000 (41.4 percent study parttime, 58.6 percent study fulltime.)

- **Faculty:** 2,500 (875 fulltime) Degrees held by faculty: doctorate (429), master's (609), licenciado (or first university degree) (1462).

- **Credentials offered:** *doctorado, maestría académica, maestría profesional, especialidad, postgrado, licenciado* (6 years), *bachiller universitario* (4 years).

- **Special programs:** *postgrado* in United States Studies, School of History and Geography. Prerequisites: English proficiency and *bachiller universitario* or *licenciado*. (See document 3.1)

Universidad del Diseño (**University of Design**)
Del Banco Nacional de Costa Rica
(San Pedro)
100 Sur y 175 al Este
San José

Established and authorized by *CONESUP* to grant credentials: July 15, 1993

Programs offered	Credential
Interior Design	*bachiller universitario*
Architecture	*licenciado*

Universidad de San José/USJ
(University of San José)
Main campus:
Avenida Central y 1era calle 33
Carretera a San Pedro
San José

Tel.: 224-9105, 224-7877
Fax: 531346

Branch campus:
200 Mts. Este y 75 Mts. Sur
de la Municipalidad de Liberia
Liberia, Guanacaste
Tel.: 66-0638

Established and authorized by *CONESUP* to grant credentials: September 17, 1992

Programs offered	Credential
Business Administrationwith emphasis in:	
General Management	*bachiller universitario, licenciado*
Banking and Finance	*bachiller universitario, licenciado*
Marketing and International Commerce	*bachiller universitario, licenciado*
Public Management	*bachiller universitario, licenciado*
Human Resources	*bachiller universitario, licenciado*
Computation	*bachiller universitario, licenciado*
Law	*bachiller universitario, licenciado*
Aquaculture Engineering	*bachiller universitario, licenciado*

Universidad Estatal a Distancia/UNED
(State University at a Distance)
Apartado 2 de Plaza González Víquez
San José
Tel: 53-2121, 24-2401
Fax: 53-4990

- **Enrollment:** 10,880

- **Faculty:** 441

Centers in: Heredia, Alajuela, Batán, Buenos Aires, Cartago, Cañas, Ciudad Neily, Jicaral, Guapiles, La Reforma, Liberia, Limón, Luján, Metropolitano (No. 2), Nicoya, Orotina, Palmares, Palmar Norte, Puntarenas, Puriscal, Quepos, San Carlos, San Isidro de El General, San Marcos, San Vito, Santa Cruz, Siquirres, Turrialba, Upala.

- **Course Requirements:** All *UNED* students are required to complete a two-part core curriculum, known as *Estudios Generales* (See Document 3.2). The parts are known as the *Ciclo Básico* and the *Ciclo Complementario*. The first cycle consists of 12 credits (4 courses): (1) Techniques of Distance Studies and Research; (2) History of Culture; 3) Language and Literature; and (4) Philosophic Perspectives of Man. The second cycle requires that students pass any two of the following courses: (1) Computer Science and Society; (2) Costa Rican History I; (3) Costa Rican History II; (4) Sociology; (5) Mathematics; (6) Introduction to the Study of Nature; and (7) History of Costa Rican Thought.

- **Credentials awarded:** *técnico* (2 years), *diplomado* (2 years), *bachiller universitario* (4 years), and *licenciatura* (5 years).
  Programs offered:
  School of Education
    Education with emphasis in:
      Educational Administration, I and II Cycles (Primary Education)
      Teacher Training
      Civic Education
      Educational Computer Science
      Early Childhood Education

School of Exact and Natural Sciences
   Agricultural Business Administration
   Health Services Administration
   Agricultural Production and Communication
   Mathematics Teaching
   Natural Sciences Teaching
   Agroindustry
   Agricultural Extension

School of Administration Sciences
   Business Administration with emphasis in:
   Accounting
   Organizational Management
   Cooperative and Associative Businesses
   Banking and Finance
   Production

Extension Program
   Library Science

Universidad Hispanoamericana
(Hispano American University)
Barrio Aranjuez
Iglesia Sta. Teresita, 100 Oeste, 100 Norte
San José
Tel: 21-1283 or 21-2261
Fax: 23-2349

Established and authorized by *CONESUP* to award credentials: July 8, 1992

Programs offered	Credential
Business Administration	*bachiller universitario, licenciado*
Business Administration, with emphasis in:	
Banking and Finance	*licenciado*
Accounting	*bachiller universitario*
Public Accounting	*licenciado, maestría*
Advertising	*bachiller universitario*
Tourism	*bachiller universitario*
Tourism with emphasis in:	
Hotel and Restaurant Administration	*licenciado*
Travel Agency Administration	*licenciado*
Health Tourism Administration	*licenciado*
Ecotourism Administration	*licenciado*
Education with emphasis in	
III Cycles (Elementary education)	*bachiller universitario*
Computer Engineering	*bachiller universitario*
Computer Engineering with emphasis in:	
Information Systems and Administration	*licenciado*

Universidad Interamericana de Costa Rica/UICR **(Interamerican University of Costa Rica)**
100 Este de la Fuente de la Hispanidad
San Pedro de Montes de Oca
Apartado 6495-1000
San José

Tel.: 234-6262 or 234-0077
Fax.: 253-8744

Established and authorized by *CONESUP* to award credentials: January 24, 1990

Programs offered	Credential
Business Administration	*licenciado*
Business Administration	
With emphasis in: Finance	*bachiller universitario**
International Trade	*bachiller universitario*
Marketing	*bachiller universitario*
Securities	*bachiller universitario*
Computation	*bachiller universitario*
Accounting	*bachiller universitario*
Economics	*bachiller universitario*
Business Administration	*maestría*
With emphasis in:	
Finance	*maestría*
Industrial Management	*maestría*
Marketing	*maestría*
Securities	*maestría*

* Note that in Costa Rica the *bachiller universitario* is frequently called *bachiller*.
See Document 3.3.

Universidad Internacional de las Américas/UIA (**International University of the Americas**)
Apartado 1447-1002
San José
Tel.: 233-5304, 222-0041, 222-3640
Fax.: 222-3216

Established and authorized by *CONESUP* to award credentials: April 1986. This urban institution was one of the first private universities in Costa Rica. Located in the center of San José, in the Aranjuez neighborhood, the *UIA* consists of the following facilities: modern classroom buildings, laboratories, three computer centers, a 12,000 volume library, audiovisual equipment, a television station, a cafeteria, a bookstore, gymnasium and athletic fields and courts. It also has a student beach club and biological reserve for fieldwork.

- **Academic Year:** The *UIA* operates on a quarter system, offering 3 quarters each academic year from January to April, May to August, and September to December.

Programs offered	Credential
Social Sciences:	
Tourism with emphasis in:	
Hotels and Restaurants	*bachiller universitario*
Transportation Methods	*bachiller universitario*
Tourist Business	*bachiller universitario*
Administration	*licenciado*
Advertising	*bachiller universitario, licenciado*
International Relations with emphasis in:	
Diplomacy/Foreign Trade	*bachiller universitario, licenciado*
Economic Sciences:	
Business Administration with emphases in:	
Finance, Management,	*bachiller universitario, licenciado, maestría*
Marketing, Advertising, Accounting,	*bachiller universitario, licenciado, maestría*
Production, Information Systems,	*bachiller universitario, licenciado, maestría*
International Trade, Computer Science	*bachiller universitario, licenciado, maestría*

Programs offered	Credential
International Trade	*bachiller universitario, licenciado, maestría*
Public Accounting	*bachiller universitario, licenciado*
Medical Sciences:	
Medicine and Surgery	*doctor**
Education and Languages:	
English with emphasis on translation	*bachiller universitario, licenciado*
Education with emphasis in preschool education (concentration in child counseling)	*bachiller universitario, licenciado*
Law	*licenciado*
Engineering:	
Systems Engineering with emphasis on Computer Center Administration and Information Systems	*bachiller universitario, licenciado, maestría*
Electromechanical Engineering	*bachiller universitario, licenciado*
Industrial Engineering	*bachiller universitario, licenciado*

* *Doctor*, when it refers to medicine or dentistry, is a first university degree in Costa Rica.

Universidad Internacional de las Américas (International University of the Americas) Regional Branch-Pérez Zeledón
Tel: 71-1516

Established and authorized by *CONESUP* to award credentials: July 26, 1989

Programs offered	Credential
Business Administration	*bachiller universitario, licenciado*
Law	*licenciado*
Systems Engineering	*bachiller universitario, maestría*
Industrial Engineering	*bachiller universitario, licenciado*

Universidad Latina de Costa Rica/UNILAT (Latin University of Costa Rica)
Main Campus:
Costado Noreste Corte Suprema de Justicia
Apartado 6397 1000
San José
Tel: 555-3833
Fax: 233-9420

Santa Cruz, Guanacaste Campus
Tel.: 680-0475

Paso Canoas Campus
Tel.: 732-2020

Ciudad Neilly Campus
Tel.: 783-4089

Pérez Zeledón Campus
Tel.: 771-2147

Established and authorized by *CONESUP* to award credentials: November 29, 1989

Programs offered	Credential
Administration with emphasis in Social Management	*licenciado*
Business Administration with emphasis in:	
Business Economics	*maestría*
Business Management	*maestría*

Programs offered	Credential
Finance and Banking	*maestría*
Social Management	*maestría*
Publicity and Marketing	*maestría*
Human Resources	*maestría, bachiller universitario, licenciado*
Accounting	*licenciado*
Public Accounting	*bachiller universitario, licenciado*
Cooperative Administration	*bachiller universitario, licenciado*
Securities	*bachiller universitario, licenciado*
Financial Entities	*bachiller universitario, licenciado*
Tourist Businesses	*bachiller universitario, licenciado*
Marketing and Sales	*bachiller universitario, licenciado*
Education	*doctorado*
Education with emphasis in:	
Educational Administration	*doctorado*
Educational Research	*doctorado*
Educational Research	*maestría*
Educational Administration	*maestría*
Educational Evaluation	*maestría*
Adult Education	*maestría*
Curriculum	*maestría*
Health Centers and Services	*maestría*
Counseling	*bachiller universitario, licenciado*
I and II Cycle (elementary education)	*bachiller universitario, licenciado*
Bilingual Teaching (English)	*bachiller universitario*
Education Administration	*bachiller universitario, licenciado*
Secondary (*enseñanza media*) Math	*bachiller universitario*
Education with emphasis in Health Education	*licenciado, maestría*
Advertising with emphasis in:	
Creativity	*maestría*
Administration and Publicity Strategy	*maestría*
Journalism	*bachiller universitario*
Collective Communication Sciences with emphasis in Public Relations	*bachiller universitario, licenciado*
Ecological Tourism	*maestría*
Environmental Conservation	*bachiller universitario, licenciado*
Systems Engineering	*bachiller universitario*
Computer Science	*licenciado*

Universidad Latinoamericana de Ciencias y Tecnología/ULACIT (Latin American University of Science and Technology)
Urbanización Tournon
Apartado 10235
San José
Tel.: 55-1050, 55-1150, Branches: San Ramón 45-5535, Limón 58-1827, Escazú 28-3154
Fax: 222-4542

Established and authorized by *CONESUP* to award credentials: June 15, 1988

Programs offered	Credential
Business Administration with emphases in:	
Finance	*bachiller universitario, licenciado*
International Trade	*bachiller universitario, licenciado*
Banking	*bachiller universitario, licenciado*
Human Resources	*bachiller universitario, licenciado*
Production	*bachiller universitario, licenciado*

Programs offered	Credential
Advertising	*bachiller universitario, licenciado*
Marketing	*bachiller universitario, licenciado*
Production Management	*bachiller universitario, licenciado*
Business Administration with emphasis in:	
Finance	*maestría*
Technology Administration	*maestría*
Marketing	*maestría*
Human Resources	*maestría*
Social Management	*maestría*
International Trade	*maestría*
Hotel Administration	*bachiller universitario*
Economic and Entrepreneurial Sciences	*doctorado*
Administration and Management Sciences	*bachiller universitario*
Accounting	*bachiller universitario*
Public Accounting	*licenciado*
Law	*bachiller universitario, licenciado, doctorado*
Industrial Engineering	*bachiller universitario, licenciado*
Computer Engineering	*bachiller universitario*
Tourism	*bachiller universitario*
Ecological Tourism	*maestría*
Tourism with an emphasis in:	
Tourism Business Administration	*licenciado*
Tourism Marketing and Planning	*licenciado*
Recreation	*licenciado*
Occupational Health	*bachiller universitario, licenciado*

Universidad Libre de Costa Rica/ULICORI **(Free University of Costa Rica)**
De la esquina sureste del Hospital Calderón Guardia
100 mts. al este
Casa N1959
San José

Established and authorized by *CONESUP* to award credentials: January 14, 1993

Programs offered	Credential
Health Services Administration	*bachiller universitario*
Health Planning	*bachiller universitario*
Medical Registry and Information Systems	*bachiller universitario*

Universidad Nacional Autónoma/UNA **(National Autonomous University)**
Apartado 86-3000
Heredia
Tel: 338-1655, 277-3900
Fax: 237-75-93

Established February 7, 1973

- **Enrollment:** 13,188

- **Faculty:** 1445

- **Organization:** The *UNA* is an autonomous public institution created in 1973. In addition to its main campus in Heredia, it offers academic programs at regional branch campuses in Brunca and Liberia.

- **Grading:** The grading scale ranges from 0 to 10, with a 7.0 being the minimum passing grade. If a student fails, an opportunity is given to take the course again the following year.

Programs offered	Credential	Years
Philosophy and Letters:		
Literature and Language Sciences		
Spanish Teaching	*bachiller universitario*	3 years
French Teaching	*bachiller universitario*	4 years
English Teaching	*bachiller universitario*	3 years
Literature and Linguistics, Spanish	*bachiller universitario*	4 years
Literature and Linguistics, English	*bachiller universitario*	4 years
Literature and Linguistics, French	*bachiller universitario*	4 years
Literature and Linguistics, Spanish	*licenciado*	5 years
Literature and Linguistics/English	*licenciado*	5 years
Literature and Linguistics/French	*licenciado*	5 years
Applied Linguistics/English emphasis	*licenciado*	5 years
Linguistics	*doctorado*	3-4 years (after *bachiller universitario*)
Religion		
Theology	*bachiller universitario*	4 years
Theology	*licenciado*	5 years
Religion Teaching	*bachiller*	4 years
Institute of Latin American Studies:		
Latin American Studies	*licenciado*	2 years (after *bachiller universitario*)
Philosophy		
Technology Teaching with concentration in:		
Accounting	*bachiller universitario*	3 years
Handicrafts	*bachiller universitario*	3 years
Typing	*bachiller universitario*	3 years
Computer science	*bachiller universitario*	3 years
Library Science	*diplomado*	(not reported)
Social Sciences		
History		
Social Studies Teaching	*bachiller universitario*	4 years
History	*bachiller universitario*	4 years
History	*licenciado*	6 years
Sociology		
Sociology	*bachiller universitario*	3 years
Sociology with concentration in:		
State in Institutional Policies	*licenciado*	5 years
Agrarian Development	*licenciado*	5 years
Urban Development	*licenciado*	5 years
Planning and Community Development		
Community Development	*asociado*	3 years
Planning	*bachiller universitario*	4 years
Planning	*licenciado*	5 years
Institute of Labor Studies:		
Labor Administration	*asociado*	3 years
Cooperative Administration	*asociado*	2 years
Professional Secretarial Science		
Secretarial Science	*asociado*	3 years
Secretarial Science with a concentration in:		
English	*bachiller universitario*	4 years
Teaching	*bachiller universitario*	4 years
International Relations		
International Relations	*bachiller universitario*	3 years

Programs offered	Credential	Years
International Relations with a concentration in:		
International Policy	_licenciado_	4 years
Economic Relations	_licenciado_	4 years
Economics		
Economics	_bachiller universitario_	4 years
Economics	_licenciado_	5 years
Economic Policy with a concentration in:		
Foreign Sector & International Relations	_maestría_	2 years
Productive Sectors	_maestría_	2 years
Human Resources and Employment	_maestría_	2 years
Natural and Exact Sciences		
Computer and Information Science		
Computer Programming	_asociado_	2.5 years
Chemistry		
Chemistry Teaching	_bachiller universitario_	3 years
Chemistry Teaching	_licenciado_	5 years
Mathematics		
Mathematics	_bachiller universitario_	3 years
Mathematics	_licenciado_	4 years
Biological Sciences		
Tropical Biology	_bachiller universitario_	4 years
Tropical Biology	_licenciado_	5 years
Marine Biology	_bachiller universitario_	4 years
Marine Biology, Aquaculture emphasis	_licenciado_	5 years
Surveying, Land Registration, and Geodesy		
Surveying and Land Registration	_asociado_	2 years
Survey Engineering and Geodesy	_bachiller universitario_	4 years
Survey Engineering and Geodesy	_licenciado_	5 years
Sciences of the Earth and Sea		
Geography		
Geography	_bachiller universitario_	3 years
Geography	_licenciado_	4 years
Agrarian Science		
Teaching of Agrarian Science	_bachiller universitario_	4 years
Agronomy	_bachiller universitario_	4 years
Agronomy	_licenciado_	5 years
Environmental Sciences		
Teaching of Environmental Science	_bachiller universitario_	3 years
Forestry	_bachiller universitario_	3 years
Forestry with concentration in:		
Wildlife Management	_licenciado_	4 years
Wildlife Areas Management	_licenciado_	4 years
Hydrography	_licenciado_	4 years
Forestry Engineer	_bachiller universitario_	4 years
Forestry Engineer	_licenciado_	5 years
Wildlife Management	_maestría_	2 years
Health Sciences		
Veterinary Science		
Veterinary Medicine	_doctor_	5 years
Tropical Veterinary Sciences Areas:		
Herd's Health and Tropical Diseases		
Regional Program	_maestría_	2 years
Sport Science		

Programs offered	Credential	Years
Physical Education	*licenciado*	4 years
Physical Education for Primary and Middle School	*bachiller universitario*	3 years
Physical Education for Secondary School with a concentration in:		
Recreation	*bachiller universitario*	3 years
Sports	*bachiller universitario*	3 years

Center for Research, Instruction, and Community Services of the Performing Arts

Programs offered	Credential	Years
Music, concentration in:		
Music Education	*bachiller universitario*	4 years
Teaching and Instrument Performance	*bachiller universitario*	4 years
Teaching and Voice	*bachiller universitario*	4 years
Teaching and Choral Directing	*bachiller universitario*	4 years
Community Production	*bachiller universitario*	4 years
Music Education	*licenciado*	2 years (after *bachiller universitario*)
Instrument	*licenciado*	2 years
Voice	*licenciado*	2 years
Choral Directing	*licenciado*	2 years
Dance		
Dance	*bachiller universitario*	4 years
Performing Arts		
Theater	*bachiller universitario*	4 years

Currently being phased out: *bachiller universitario* programs in Instrument, Voice, Teaching: Instrument and Choral, and Community Promotion.

Center for Research and Instruction in Education

Programs offered	Credential	Years
Education for Primary/ Middle School	*asociado*	2 years
Education, Primary/Middle School, in Problems of Rural Areas	*asociado*	3 years
Education with emphasis in Industrial Arts Teaching Degree in Primary/Middle School	*asociado, bachiller universitario*	3 years
Science of Education with specialization in:		
Educational Guidance	*bachiller universitario*	3 years
Preschool	*bachiller universitario*	3 years
Educational Administration	*bachiller universitario*	3 years
Adult Education	*bachiller universitario*	3 years
Learning Problems	*bachiller universitario*	3 years
Pedagogy of Communication	*bachiller universitario*	3 years
Home Economics	*bachiller universitario*	3 years
Primary and Middle School	*bachiller universitario*	3 years
Primary and Middle School Mathematics	*bachiller universitario*	3 years
Primary and Middle School Spanish	*bachiller universitario*	3 years
Science of Education with specialization in:		
Education Guidance	*licenciado*	4 years
Preschool	*licenciado*	4 years
Educational Administration	*licenciado*	4 years
Pedagogy of Communication	*licenciado*	4 years
Center for General Studies (Humanities)	*licenciado*	4 years
Humanities	*certificado*	1 year

A 2-year (6 trimester) postgraduate *maestría* in the social sciences, with an emphasis in regional integration, is offered in conjunction with the *Facultad Latinoamericana de Ciencias Sociales/FLACSO*. The *UNA* also offers Women's Studies programs through its interdisciplinary Institute of Women's Studies/IIEM, population studies at the Social Research Institute, the Volcanic and Seismological Observatory of Costa Rica/OVSICORI, a sports medicine institute, and a child care institute.

Universidad Nazarena/UNAZA (Nazarene University)
Alto de Guadalupe
100 al Este de Proursa
Carretera a Ipis de Coronado

Established and authorized by *CONESUP* to award credentials: October 29, 1992

Programs offered	Credential
Ecclesiastic Resource Administration	*bachiller universitario, licenciado*
Concentrations:	
Pastoral	*licenciado*
Religion Teaching	*licenciado*
Theology	*bachiller universitario, licenciado*
Religion with emphasis in library science	*maestría*

Universidad Panamericana/UPA (Pan American University)
Calle 23 Avenidas Central y 1ra.
Apartado 1106 Código 2050
San José
Tel.: 221-5498
Fax: 223-3358

Established and authorized by *CONESUP* to award credentials: December 16, 1988

College	Programs offered	Credential
Colegio Isaac Newton	Administration	*bachiller universitario*
Contiguo a Plaza del Sol	Business Administration	*licenciado*
Curridabat	Basic Sciences of Civil Engineering	*bachiller universitario*
	Civil Engineering	*licenciado*
	Industrial Engineering	*licenciado*
	Industrial Engineering	*bachiller universitario*
	Advertising	*bachiller universitario, licenciado*
	Public Relations	*bachiller universitario, licenciado*
Colegio Justiniano	Law	*bachiller universitario, licenciado*
De la esquina suroeste del	Human Resources	*bachiller universitario, licenciado*
Museo Nacional		
75 mts. Sur y 50 mts. Oeste		
San José		
Colegio Magister	Business Administration	*bachiller universitario, licenciado*
Barrio La California	Pre-school Education	*bachiller universitario*
Contiguo al Cine Magaly	English	*bachiller universitario*
San José	Computer Systems	*bachiller universitario*
Colegio San Agustín	Administration with emphasis in	
Barrio La Cruz	Accounting and Finance	*bachiller universitario, licenciado*
detrás del Centro	Architecture	*bachiller universitario, licenciado*
Comerical del Sur	Advertising Design	*bachiller universitario, maestría*
San José		

Universidad Panamericana/UPA (Pan American University)
San Carlos Branch

Established and authorized by *CONESUP* to award credentials: February 21, 1990

College	Programs offered	Credential
Colegio Isaac Newton	Advertising	*bachiller, universitario, licenciado*
Colegio Justiniano	Law	*bachiller universitario, licenciado*
Colegio Magister	Administration	*bachiller universitario*
	Business Administration	*licenciado*
	Pre-School Education	*bachiller universitario*
	English	*bachiller universitario*
	Computer Systems	*bachiller universitario*
Colegio San Agustín	Administration with emphasis in	
	Accounting and Finance	*bachiller universitario, licenciado*
	Architecture	*bachiller universitario, licenciado*
	Advertising Design	*bachiller universitario, maestría*

Parauniversities

The following institutions function as "parauniversities" or other postsecondary institutions offering technical degrees, adult education courses, certificates, and diplomas. They are generally recognized by the *Consejo Superior de Educación*, but readers are advised to verify this information directly with the institutions.

American Business Academy
Apartado 3818-1000
Calle Central
75 m. al sur del Cine Rex
San José
Tel.: 222-4211
Fax: 222-4031

Programs offered	Credential
Executive Bilingual Secretary	*diplomado*
Executive Secretary in Spanish	*diplomado*
Business Administration	*diplomado*
Accounting Sciences	*diplomado*
Computer Science	*diplomado*
Internal Auditing	*diplomado*
Bilingual Secretary	*técnico*
Bilingual Office Worker	*técnico*
Secretary	*técnico*
Office Worker	*técnico*
Tourism	*técnico*

Colegio Universitario de Cartago (University College of Cartago)
Barrio El Molino
Avenida 5, Calle 3
Cartago
Tels.: 551-9223/551-4353/551-3321
Fax: 551-5066

Established in 1977.

***Instituto Latinoamericano de Computación/ILAC* (Latin American Institute of Computation)**
Avenida Central
25 m. oeste del Hotel Balmoral
San José
Tel.: 255-4545, 222-2150

- **Organization:** The *ILAC* offers technical training on the tertiary level, offering 8 month computer courses, 2 year *diplomado* programs, and 1 year *técnico* programs. For students who complete the 2 year programs, *ILAC* has an agreement with the *Universidad Latinoamericana de Ciencias y Tecnología/ULACIT,* in which students may receive transfer credit at the university for *ILAC* courses.

Programs offered	Credential	Duration
Computer Operator	*operador de computadoras*	8 months
Administrative Computation	*diplomado*	2 years
Business Administration	*diplomado*	2 years
Computerized Accounting	*diplomado*	2 years
Computer Science Secretary	*diplomado*	2 years
Programming	*técnico*	1 year
Computer Office Worker	*técnico*	1 year
Computer Accounting Assistant	*técnico*	

***Instituto Superior de Administración de Empresa/ISAE* (Higher Institute of Business Administration)**
Frente al Parque de Juegos de la Dolorosa
San José
Tel.: 233-9868, 223-3779
Fax: 233-9824

The *ISAE* has an agreement with the Universidad Panamericana which allows the coursework of graduates to be transferred to *licenciado* and *bachiller universitario* programs at the university.

Programs offered	Credential
Accounting	*diplomado*
Accounting Assistant	(Non-degree)

Postsecondary Programs (operated by foreign or international organizations)

***Centro Agronómico Tropical de Investigación y Enseñanza/CATIE* (Tropical Agriculture Research and Higher Education Center)**
Turrialba
Tel.: 556-64-31, 556-01-69
Fax: 556-1533

Established 1942: *CATIE* evolved from the Interamerican Institute for Agricultural Sciences/*IICA*), which was founded by the Organization of American States. It was given a hemispheric mandate to provide education and training and to carry out research in agriculture, livestock production, and forestry for regional development. In 1960, *IICA*'s office of directors moved to San José, and the Turrialba site was renamed the Center for Education and Research/*CEI*). In 1970, *CEI* became the Tropical Center for Education and Research, and in 1973, the process culminated in the creation of *CATIE*, as part of an agreement between *IICA* and the government of Costa Rica. The institution's member countries are: Costa Rica, El Salvador, Guatemala, Honduras, Nicaragua, Mexico, Panama, the Dominican Republic and Venezuela.

- **Academic year:** Degree programs are 8 quarters of approximately 12 weeks (a total of 2 years), beginning in January. Coursework is conducted in the first 4 quarters, and the second 4 quarters are dedicated to research for the thesis.

- **Faculty:** Approximately 50 doctoral and 70 master's level faculty members.

- **Admission:** Candidates must hold a Bachelor's of Science degree or its equivalent in biological science, agronomy, forestry, or related areas, awarded by a recognized institution of higher education. Preference is given to applicants under 35 years of age. Reference letters and an entrance examination are also required.

- **Credentials Awarded:** Current degree programs emerged from the school's original 1944 Master's Program. According to *CATIE*, the Interamerican Board of Agriculture/*JIA*) has granted the institution the power to confer the title of *Magister Scientiae*, which is the official name of the credential awarded. It is commonly referred to as a master's degree or *maestría*. *CATIE* offers degrees in the following areas:

  1. Sustainable Agricultural Production Systems emphasizing: a. Tropical Crops; b. Plant Protection; c. Agroforestry Systems

  2. Integrated Management of Natural Resources emphasizing: a. Watershed Management; b. Biodiversity Management and Conservation; and c. Tropical Forest Management and Silviculture.

Escuela de Agricultura de la Región Tropical Húmeda/EARTH **(Agricultural School of the Humid Tropical Region)**
Urbanización El Prado
Tel.: 253-5454, 255-2000
Fax: 253-4597

- **Organization:** *EARTH* offers one 4-year postecondary program in agronomy, with an emphasis in the Humid Tropics (*Ingeniero agronómico con énfasis en los trópicos húmedos*). The year is divided into 3 trimesters, from January to December. Students live and study in the field; they are given one month of vacation between trimesters.

Instituto Centroamericano de Administración de Empresas/INCAE **(Central American Institute of Business Administration)**
Dirección Ejecutiva (Executive Offices)
200 norte esquina noroeste del ICE
Sabana
Tel.: 231-1775, 231-2617
Fax: 231-4705

Alajuela campus:
Apartado 960-40050
Alajuela
Tel.: 441-2255
Fax: 433-9101

Established in 1964 at the behest of the Central American business community, *INCAE* is a private, multinational institution of higher education dedicated to teaching, research, and assistance in business administration in Latin America. It has received technical assistance from the U.S. Agency of International Development and the Harvard University School of Business. *INCAE* has a sister campus in Managua, Nicaragua.

In addition to its three master's degree programs, *INCAE* offers eight non-degree business courses which vary in length from 2 weeks to 1 year:

Programs offered	Credential	Duration
Business Administration	Master	2 years
Executive	Master	1.5 years
Business Economics	Master	2 years

Universidad para la Paz **(Peace University)**
Ciudad Colon, Mora
Mailing address: Apartado 199-1250
Escazú
Tel: 249-1072, 249-1512, 249-1513
Fax: 249-1929

Established by the United Nations General Assembly on December 5, 1980, the *Universidad para la Paz* is a private, international university. According to the university's literature, the institution is governed by a council made up of 16 members, including the secretary general of the U.N., the director of UNESCO, 10 representatives of the international academic community, two Costa Rican representatives, the rector of the United Nations University, the executive director of UNITAR, and the rector of the *Universidad para la Paz*.

In the United Nations resolution establishing the university, it is described as "a specialized international institution for postgraduate studies, research and dissemination of knowledge specifically aimed at training for peace within the system of the United Nations University..." Graduate level programs of study include the following:

Program of Study	Credential	Duration
Natural Resources and Sustainable Development	Master	2 years
International Relations	Master	1 year

The university also operates a television station at its Gandhi Center of Communication, opened in 1987, and a radio station called Radio Paz Internacional (RPI).

(Note: See Glossary overleaf)

Glossary

A la fecha la oficina de registro no cuenta con dicha información (X). Information unavailable

Anual (Año). Yearly or Year-long

Aplazado por no haber obtenido en el examen final de la nota mínima establecida por la escuela F. Failed for not having obtained the minimum grade established by the school on the final exam.

Aprobado (A or AP). Passed

Asociado. Associate

Bachiller Universitario. First university degree (also called *Bachiller or Bachillerato*) (Not to be confused with secondary credential by the same name)

Carrera Corta. Short program, usually leading to an intermediate degree

Certificado. Certificate

Ciclo Básico. Basic Cycle; first section of required courses in General Studies program

Ciclo Complementario. Complementary Cycle, second section of required courses in General Studies program.

Colegio. Generally refers to secondary school; also used in Costa Rica at postsecondary level to mean "college" (in the U.S. definition of faculty within a university or undergraduate institution)

Cursado (C). Course taken and completed

Curso Incompleto (CI). Course incomplete

Diplomado. Diploma, may also be called *diploma* or *diplomado universitario*

Doctor/ Doctorado. Doctorate

Duración del Curso (Dur. Cur.). Course Duration

Especial (Esp.). Special

Especialidad/Especialización. Specialty/Specialization

Estudios Generales. General Studies, core of basic courses required of all students

Equiparación de Curso. (EQ)

Exento (EX or EXT). Exempt

Grado. First university degree; also means level (e.g. *grado académico* is academic level)

Incompleto (IN or INC). Incomplete

Ingeniero. Engineer

Interrupción de Estudios (I or IT). Interruption of Studies

Licenciado/Licenciatura. Licenciate

Maestría. Master's degree

Matriculada (MA). Currently enrolled

Modalidad de Estudio (Mod. Est). Type of Study

No Se Presentó a Examen (NSP). Did not take exam

Pensum. List of required courses and prerequisites for a specific program; also called *plan de estudios* (study plan)

Perdido Sin Derecho a Examen Extraordinario (P or PE). Failed without possibility of taking special examination
Postgrado (also spelled *posgrado*). Graduate degree

Pregrado. Preuniversity level degree

Profesor/ Profesorado. Teacher/Teaching degree

Promedio Ponderado. Grade point average*

Regular (Reg.). Regular

Reconocida (RE or REC). Recognized

Reprobada (R). Failed

Reprobada por Ausencias (RPA). Failed for non-attendance

Retiro Injustificado (RI). Unexcused withdrawal

Retiro Justificado (RJ). Justified withdrawal

Satisfactorio (S). Satisfactory

Semestral (Sem.). Semesterly

Suficiencia (Suf.). Equivalency

Técnico. Technician

Técnico Superior. Higher level technician

Tutoria (Tut.) Tutorial

---

* Note: The grade point average is calculated by multiplying the grade obtained by the number of credits each course is worth. The sum of this product is divided among the total number of credits taken. In calculating the grade point average, the grades PE and RI have a numerical value of 5.5. The symbols AP, EQ, RE, RJ, IN, and IT are not factored into this formula

```
UNIVERSIDAD DE COSTA RICA                                    No. ▪▪▪▪▪▪

OFICINA DE REGISTRO

                            CERTIFICA QUE:
NOMBRE:                                                   EXP. No.:
                                                          ▪▪▪▪▪▪
DIRECCION:

FECHA DE NACIMIENTO:          No. DE CEDULA          NOTA DE ADMISION:
        21/09/68                                              504
CARRERA QUE SIGUE:                      Sample Document
             BACH Y LIC EN GEOGRAFIA

CONDICION DEL ESTUDIANTE:
             REGULAR              PROMEDIO PONDERADO TOTAL:  7.36
```

```
     CURSO LAS SIGUIENTES ASIGNATURAS EN LA UNIVERSIDAD DE COSTA RICA:
   RECIN- CICLO                                 CALIFICACION CRE- MOD DUR TIPO
    TO    MATRIC.        ASIGNATURAS            ORD.  EXT. DITOS EST CUR NOTA
   ---------------------------------------------------------------------------
   **   1-1988 ************************************** ****  ****  **** *** ***
   11   EG0123 CURSO INTEGRADO DE HUMANIDADES    07.0        12.0 REG ANU
   11   MA0125 MATEMATICA ELEMENTAL              PE          **** REG SEM
   **   2-1989 ************************************** ****  ****  **** *** ***
   11   FS0118 FISICA I                          RI          **** REG SEM
   11   MA0125 MATEMATICA ELEMENTAL              PE          **** REG SEM
   11   QU0100 QUIMICA GENERAL I                 PE          **** REG SEM
   11   QU0101 LABORATORIO DE QUIMICA GENERAL I  07.0        01.0 REG SEM
   **   1-1990 ************************************** ****  ****  **** *** ***
   11   EG0061 APRECIACION CINEMATOGRAFICA       09.0        02.0 REG ANU
   11   HG1000 HISTORIA DE LAS INSTITUCIONES DE COSTA **** **** **** *** ***
               RICA                              07.0        04.0 REG ANU
   11   MA0125 MATEMATICA ELEMENTAL              07.0        02.0 REG ANU
   **   2-1990 ************************************** ****  ****  **** *** ***
   11   EG0018 PROBLEMAS ECOLOGICOS              08.5        03.0 REG SEM
   11   HG0101 ANALISIS  GEOGRAFICO 1            07.5        03.0 REG SEM
   **   1-1991 ************************************** ****  ****  **** *** ***
   11   HG0103 GEOGRAFIA MUNDIAL                 07.0        03.0 REG SEM
   11   HG0204 GEOGRAFIA CULTURAL                07.5        03.0 REG SEM
   11   LM1030 INGLES INTENSIVO I                PE          **** REG SEM
   11   XE0156 INTRODUCCION A LA ECONOMIA        06.5 ****   **** REG SEM
   **   2-1991 ************************************** ****  ****  **** *** ***
   11   G 0111 FUNDAMENTOS DE GEOLOGIA           08.0        04.0 REG SEM
   11   HG0203 GEOGRAFIA DE AMERICA LATINA       09.0        03.0 REG SEM
   11   HG0205 CLIMATOLOGIA                      07.0        03.0 REG SEM
   11   HG0215 CARTOGRAFIA BASICA                07.0        03.0 REG SEM
   11   XE0156 INTRODUCCION A LA ECONOMIA        07.5        04.0 REG SEM
   **   1-1992 ************************************** ****  ****  **** *** ***
   11   HG0207 GEOGRAFIA DE AMERICA CENTRAL      07.0        03.0 REG SEM
   11   HG0305 GEOMORFOLOGIA                     07.0        03.0 REG SEM
   11   HG0306 GEOPEDOLOGIA                      07.0        03.0 REG SEM
   11   HG0307 GEOGRAFIA POLITICA                08.5        03.0 REG SEM
   11   HG0315 GEOGRAFIA DE LA POBLACION         08.0        03.0 REG SEM
   11   XS0401 ESTADISTICA PARA HISTORIADORES    RI          **** REG SEM
   **   2-1992 ************************************** ****  ****  **** *** ***
   ---------------------------------------------------------------------------
   ---------------------------------------------------------------------------
                      PASA A FOLIO INMEDIATO SUPERIOR
```

Document 3.1.1 Partial transcript for the *Universidad De Costa Rica/UCR*. (NOTE: Students may complete only the *bachiller universitario* or continue on for the licenciatura. Some courses last a semester ("sem") while others last a year ("anu").

UNIVERSIDAD DE COSTA RICA   No. ⸴⸴⸴⸴⸴

OFICINA DE REGISTRO

VIENE DE FOLIO INMEDIATO INFERIOR

| NOMBRE: | ⸴⸴⸴⸴ BORRAS MARVIN———————————————— | EXP. No.: | ⸴⸴⸴⸴⸴ |

DIRECCION:

| FECHA DE NACIMIENTO: | 21/09/68 | No. DE CEDULA ⸴⸴⸴⸴⸴⸴⸴⸴ | NOTA DE ADMISION: 504 |

CARRERA QUE SIGUE: BACH Y LIC EN GEOGRAFIA

CONDICION DEL ESTUDIANTE: REGULAR   PROMEDIO PONDERADO TOTAL: 007.36

```
RECIN- CICLO                              CALIFICACION CRE- MOD DUR TIPO
  TO   MATRIC.        ASIGNATURAS         ORD.  EXT. DITOS EST CUR NOTA
------------------------------------------------------------------------
  11  HG0206 GEOGRAFIA ECONOMICA          08.0        03.0 REG SEM
  11  HG0308 BIOGEOGRAFIA       Sample Document PE    **** REG SEM
  11  HG0309 GEOGRAFIA RURAL              08.0        03.0 REG SEM
  11  HG0320 GEOGRAFIA HISTORICA          08.0        03.0 REG SEM
  11  HG0415 GEOGRAFIA DE LA ENERGIA      09.0        03.0 REG SEM
  11  XS0248 ESTADISTICA PARA CIENCIAS SOCIALES I 07.5 03.0 REG SEM
  **  1-1993 ************************************** **** **** **** *** ***
  11  EF7161 ACTIVIDAD DEPORTIVA: SISTEMA  **** **** **** *** ***
             PREPARACION FISICA PRINCIPIANTES HOMBRES AP 00.0 REG SEM
  11  HG0317 INVESTIGACION GEOGRAFICA     07.0        03.0 REG SEM
  11  HG0401 GEOGRAFIA URBANA             07.5        03.0 REG SEM
  11  HG0402 HIDROGEOGRAFIA               08.0        04.0 REG SEM
  11  SR0008 SEM. REAL. NAC.1: DESARROLLO COMUNAL 10.0 02.0 REG SEM
  **  2-1993 ************************************** **** **** **** *** ***
  11  HG0308 BIOGEOGRAFIA                 08.5        03.0 REG SEM
  11  HG0412 SENSORES REMOTOS             07.5        04.0 REG SEM
  11  HG0413 PROY. INVEST. EN GEOGRAFIA   09.5        04.0 REG SEM
  11  LM1030 INGLES INTENSIVO I           RJ          **** REG SEM
  11  LM2003 FRANCES BASICO I             RJ          **** REG SEM
  11  SR0022 SEMINARIO DE REALIDAD NACIONAL 2: PRO **** **** **** *** ***
             DUCCION Y DESARROLLO        08.5         02.0 REG SEM
  **  3-1993 ************************************** **** **** **** *** ***
  11  EF6151 ACTIVIDAD DEPORTIVA: HATHA YOGA **** **** **** *** ***
             PRINCIPIANTES MIXTO          AP          00.0 REG SEM
  **  1-1994 ************************************** **** **** **** *** ***
  11  AS1103 INTRODUCCION A LA SOCIOLOGIA I MA       03.0 REG SEM
  11  HG0409 ECOLOGIA TROPICAL            MA          04.0 REG SEM
  11  HG0411 EL PENSAMIENTO GEOGRAFICO CONTEMPORANEO MA 03.0 TUT SEM
  11  HG0414 INTRODUCCION ORDENAMIENTO TERRITORIAL MA 04.0 TUT SEM
  11  HG0521 MODELOS GEOGRAFICOS AVANZADOS MA        04.0 REG SEM
  11  HG2510 GEOGRAFIA REGIONAL DE COSTA RICA MA     03.0 REG SEM
  11  LM1030 INGLES INTENSIVO I           MA          04.0 REG SEM
------------------------------------------------------------------------

           PASA A FOLIO INMEDIATO SUPERIOR
```

Document 3.1.2 (see previous)

- 24

UNIVERSIDAD ESTATAL A DISTANCIA
Vicerrectoría Ejecutiva
Oficina de Registro

No. CERTIFICACION:

No. CARNE:

UNED

Página :   1

CERTIFICA

Que   Cédula

CURSO LAS SIGUIENTES ASIGNATURAS EN LA UNIVERSIDAD ESTATAL A DISTANCIA

AÑOS	ASIGNATURAS	CREDITOS	CALIFICACIONES
91 1			
00197	PLANEAMIENTO DIDACTICO	3,00	8,00
91 2			
00108	RECURSOS AUDIOVISUALES	3,00	7,50
00328	COMUNICACION ESCRITA	3,00	7,50
92 1			
00105	LITERATURA INFANTIL	3,00	PERDIDA
00117	ORIENTACION EDUCATIVA	3,00	8,00
00125	DIDACTICA DE LAS CIENCIAS NATURALES	3,00	7,00
00148	PRINCIPIOS Y TECNICAS DE EVALUACION	3,00	8,00
92 2			
00101	EDUCACION COSTARRICENSE	3,00	9,00
00111	EDUCACION PARA LA SALUD	3,00	7,50
00120	MATEMATICA ELEMENTAL I	3,00	N.S.P.
00140	ELEMENTOS DE BIOLOGIA HUMANA	3,00	8,00
93 1			
00119	TECNICAS DEL HOGAR	3,00	9,50
00124	DIDACTICA DE LOS ESTUDIOS SOCIALES	3,00	8,50
00131	HISTORIA Y EDUCACION CIVICA COSTARR	3,00	8,00
00146	DIDACTICA DE LA LECTO ESCRITURA	4,00	7,50
00704	PSICOLOGIA DEL NIÑO EN EDAD ESCOLAR	3,00	8,50
93 2			
00102	ELEMENTOS DE BIBLIOTECOLOGIA	3,00	7,00
00122	DIDACTICA DE ESPAÑOL	3,00	8,00
00123	DIDACTICA DE LA MATEMATICA	3,00	8,50
00144	DIDACTICA GENERAL I	3,00	7,50
94 1			

Continúa...

- ORIGINAL - ESTUDIANTE -   SISTEMAS / X F Z / 7-9-90

Document 3.2.1 A transcript of currently enrolled student at the *Universidad Estatal a Distancia/UNED*

UNIVERSIDAD ESTATAL A DISTANCIA
Vicerrectoría Ejecutiva
Oficina de Registro

No. CERTIFICACION: ⊔⊔⊔⊔⊔⊔

No. CARNE: ,⊔⊔⊔⊔⊔⊔

Continuación...
Página : 2

CERTIFICA

Que ....   Cédula : ⊔ -⊔⊔⊔⊔ ⊔⊔⊔⊔

CURSO LAS SIGUIENTES ASIGNATURAS EN LA UNIVERSIDAD ESTATAL A DISTANCIA

AÑOS	ASIGNATURAS	CREDITOS	CALIFICACIONES
94 1			
00105	LITERATURA INFANTIL	3,00	EN CURSO
00121	GEOGRAFIA DE COSTA RICA	3,00	EN CURSO
00132	MUSICA I Y II CICLO	3,00	EN CURSO
00179	PRACTICA DOCENTE III (PLAN DE EMERG	6,00	EN CURSO

LAS CALIFICACIONES SE AJUSTAN A LA ESCALA DE 0 A 10 SIENDO LA MINIMA DE
APROBACIαN DE SIETE (7.00)
Nota:Ret.Auto.=Retiro Autorizado, Ret. Just.=Retiro Justificado, NSP.=No se
Presento, O=Ordinaria, V=Verano, S=Suficiencia.
SE EXTIENDE LA PRESENTE A SOLICITUD DEL INTERESADO EL 04 DE Mayo   DE
1994 .NULA SIN EL SELLO BLANCO DE LA OFICINA DE REGISTRO Y LA FIRMA DEL
JEFE DE LA MISMA . SE AGREGAN Y CANCELAN LOS RESPECTIVOS TIMBRES DE LEY.
ULTIMA LINEA

MBA. PABLO RAMIREZ MENDOZA.   SRA. LIDIETTE CALVO VALVERDE.
JEFE OFICINA REGISTRO.   CONTROL DE ACTAS.

- ORIGINAL - ESTUDIANTE -   SISTEMAS/XPZ/7-9-90

Document 3.2.2 (see previous)

RE-24

UNIVERSIDAD ESTATAL A DISTANCIA
Vicerrectoría Ejecutiva
· Oficina de Registro

No. CERTIFICACION: ՕՕＬＬＪＵ

No. CARNE:

UNED

CERTIFICA

Que

SE LE RECONOCIERON LAS SIGUIENTES ASIGNATURAS EN LA UNIVERSIDAD ESTATAL
DISTANCIA:

Sample Document

ESTA ES UNA AMPLIACION A LA CERTIFICACION FOLIOS 032119 Y 032120.

AÑOS	ASIGNATURAS	CREDITOS	CALIFICACIONES
---	CICLO BASICO	12	REC

Se extiende la presente a solicitud de la interesada a los cinco días del
mes de mayo de mil novecientos noventa y cuatro. Nula sin el sello blanco
de la Oficina de Registro y la firma del Jefe de la misma. Se agregan y
cancelan los respectivos timbres de de Ley.─
─────────────────────────────ULTIMA LINEA─────────────────────────────

MBA. PABLO RAMIREZ MENDOZA
JEFE OFICINA DE REGISTRO

LIDIETTE CALVO VALVERDE
CONTROL DE ACTAS

am.

- ORIGINAL - ESTUDIANTE -   SISTEMAS / X P Z / 7-9-80

Document 3.2.3 (see previous)

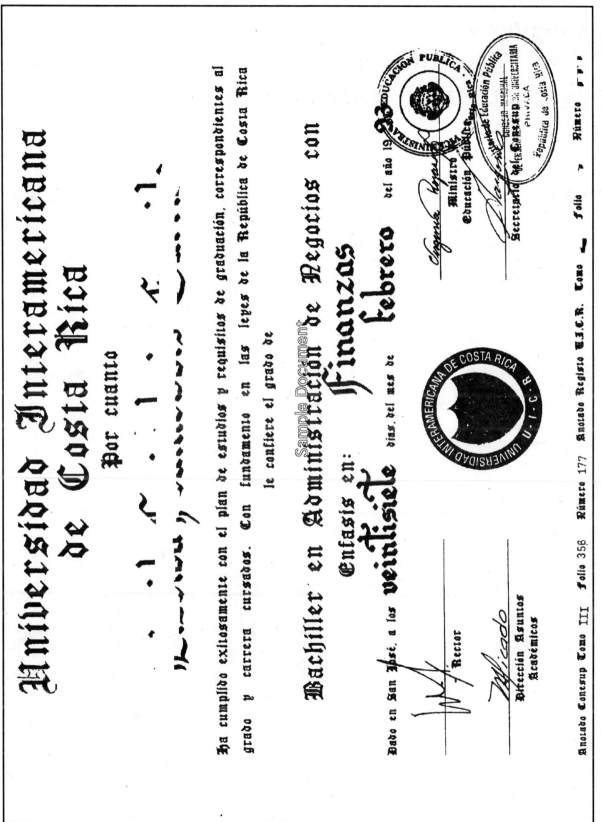

Document 3.3 This *bachiller* from the *Universidad Interamericana de Costa Rica* is a postsecondary credential and should not be confused with the secondary level degree of the same name.

Chapter 4
The Educational System of El Salvador

The Country

El Salvador, located on the Pacific Coast of Central America among Nicaragua, Guatemala, and Honduras, is the most densely populated country in the region. It spent the 1980s fighting a divisive, costly war which wreaked havoc on the nation's civic life. Among the casualties of the war were the destruction of the *Universidad de El Salvador* (the national university) on two occasions, and the assassination of several faculty members at the Jesuit *Universidad Centroamericana*. However, since the signing of peace accords in 1992, Salvadoran society has begun the process of healing and rebuilding, and improvements are visible throughout the nation.

Postsecondary Education

The 1980s witnessed the establishment of a plethora of small, independent centers of higher learning in El Salvador. The country is the smallest in the Western Hemisphere in geographical land mass, but it boasts the largest number of universities on the isthmus at 38, and that number does not include regional branches or campuses. The largest and most prestigious institutions continue to be the public *Universidad de El Salvador/UES* and the private Jesuit *Universidad Centroamericana/UCA*, but students are increasingly seeking degree programs in the newer private universities. Many of the private universities that were founded in this period have flourished, with some expanding in the areas of computer sciences and business administration. There are also 21 non-university institutions of higher education, which offer technical postsecondary programs.

This boom in postsecondary education has prompted much debate in El Salvador. The higher education community finds itself in a transitional state, as the Salvadoran Congress debates a "Law of Higher Education" that would regulate and standardize the country's educational system. The law would establish norms and standards for postsecondary institutions, and would contain guidelines regarding curriculum, required facilities, number of

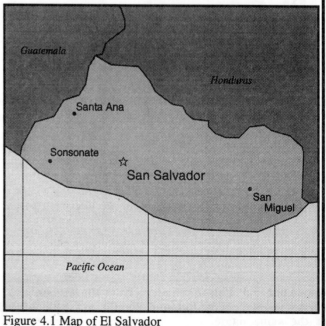

Official name: Republic of El Salvador

Area: 21,476 square kilometers/8,260 square miles (about the size of Massachusetts)

Capital: San Salvador

Population: 5 million

Annual growth rate: 3 percent

Noun and adjective: Salvadoran(s)

Ethnic groups: Mestizo 89%; indigenous 10%; other 1%

Religion: Primarily Catholic, with a growing Protestant minority

Language: Spanish

Education: Years compulsory-6; Attendance - 82%; Literacy-65%

(Source: U.S. State Department *Background Notes*)

Figure 4.1 Map of El Salvador

faculty, library holdings, etc. that may affect the future accreditation of a number of colleges and universities in the country. It is difficult to predict which private institutions will flourish in the coming years, or even which can be expected to survive.

Credentials

The following are postsecondary certificates, degrees, and titles. While the original source is the 1987 PIER report, the Salvadoran Ministry of Education updated the data in 1994. Most programs require that students successfully complete a pre-established number of credits, which are called *unidades valorativas,* and abbreviated *u.v.* The *bachiller* is the uniform secondary diploma most commonly accepted for university admission. It contains a common academic core with special areas of concentration.

Enfermería Graduada, **Diplomatura en Enfermería (graduate or diploma in nursing):** Generally 3-year degrees, these replace the 2-year Nursing Aide program. The *Enfermeria Graduada* (Graduate in Nursing) degree is awarded to professionals who can "identify and satisfy" people's health needs.

The *Enfermero Diplomado* **(diploma in nursing)** is awarded to professionals with theoretical/practical knowledge of health sciences, who are capable of planning, organizing, executing, and evaluating health-related situations and strategies.

Técnico/Profesor **(technician/teacher, non university-level institutions):** Although this title no longer exists, teacher training continues to take place within the technical area of higher education. There are technical and degree programs lasting 2-3 years in both nonuniversity and university settings. The difference between their graduates is that students from postsecondary nonuniversity institutions usually have more practical training than the university graduates.

Técnico **(technician, university degree):** Title awarded in many professions after 3 years of university study, sometimes the first 3 years of a *licenciatura* in the same field. Students may go directly into employment or continue in a *licenciado* program.

Bachiller Mayor: A 2-year university-level degree awarded by the *Universidad Dr. J.M. Delgado.*

Profesor/ Profesorado **(teacher, from a university):** A 3-year university degree and teaching qualification which prepares students for primary, secondary, and special education school teaching. It is designed to lead to employment, but students often continue with advanced standing toward a *licenciatura.*

Bibliotecario **(librarian):** A 3-year degree in library science offered by the *Universidad de El* Salvador.

Técnico Avanzado **(advanced technician):** This degree consists of 3 years of study. Students are awarded the *técnico* degree after the second year, and the *avanzado* distinction after 1 additional year.

Licenciado: First university degree varying in length from 5-5.5 years. Requires a thesis or graduation project. Minimum qualification for teaching at the university level; candidates are required to take at least 140 *u.v.*

Ingeniero, Arquitecto: **(engineer, architect):** First professional degree programs, requiring 5 to 5.5 and 5.5 years respectively. A minimum of 180 *u.v.* required to complete the program.

Doctor en Medicina/Médico **(medical doctor),** *Doctor en Odontología* **(Dentist),** *Cirujano Dental* **(dental surgeon),** *Abogado* **(lawyer);** first and only degrees offered in fields of medicine, dentistry, or law. Each requires 210 *u.v.* and 5-7 years of fulltime study.

Profesorado Universitario **(university teacher):** A 1-year postgraduate diploma in university teaching awarded by the *Universidad Francisco Gavidia.*

Maestría **(master's):** Usually a 2-year post-*licenciatura* program, which requires a thesis. Under the new law, would require at least 64 *u.v.*

Doctor, Doctorado **(doctorate):** Not previously defined, see proposed guidelines outlined in the new law (below).

New Higher Education Law

If the new law of higher education passes, it may alter the number and quality of postsecondary institutions significantly. At this writing, the law is on the verge of passing after years of debate. Its creation, a cooperative effort among the private and public universities, is symbolic of the nation's desire for reconciliation after a decade of political and social divisions. Its implementation would place control of higher education in the hands of a consortium of institutions that represent a broad spectrum of political ideologies, and would have the responsibility of ensuring that established standards of quality in education would be upheld.

Standards and Definitions Proposed

Degrees that may be conferred, according to the proposed law, are the *licenciado, arquitecto,* and *ingeniero* for undergraduates. There are two degrees awarded at the graduate level, the *maestría* and the *doctorado.*

Transfer credits: The law authorizes institutions to grant equivalent credit for academic studies undertaken at different colleges and universities, in El Salvador and abroad. However, the grades for these classes are not recorded, they are noted as "*aprobada*" or "*reprobada*" (passed or failed).

Technical education is defined as studies beyond secondary school (*educación media*) that do not reach the level of *licenciado, ingeniero,* or *arquitecto.* This category consists of 2-year programs which require a minimum of 64 *u.v.* (credits). Institutions that only offer such programs are called *Instituciones de Educación*

Tecnológica (Institutions of Technological Education), not universities. (For more information about these institutions, see listing below).

Undergraduate Degrees

Undergraduate degrees are also defined in the proposed law as follows: the *licenciado* is no less than a 5-year degree, which must contain at least 170 *u.v.* *Ingeniero* and *arquitecto* degree programs must include at least 180 *u.v.* Only students with the three degrees may proceed to graduate study under the proposed legislation.

Professional credentials such as lawyer (*abogado*), architect (*arquitecto*), and medical doctor (*médico*) are commonly first university degrees as well.

Graduate Degrees

Graduate degrees are also assigned minimum standards by the law. The *maestría* requires 2 years of study, a minimum of 64 *u.v.*, a scientific research project (usually a thesis), and comprehensive oral examination or 12 additional *u.v.* from the plan of study. The *doctorado* requires 266 *u.v.* total. If it is undertaken after completion of one of the above-mentioned undergraduate degrees, it requires a minimum of 3 additional full-time years of study, in-cluding 96 *u.v.* When it follows as *maestría*, 32 *u.v.* must be completed. Other graduate degrees that may be created will also require at least 32 *u.v.* beyond the *licenciado* under the new education law.

Graduation: Students must earn at least 30 *u.v.* in the institution in which studies are completed, and must obtain a cumulative grade point average of at least 7.0.

Institutions of Higher Education

The *Consejo de Educación Superior* determines whether or not an institution may be recognized by the Ministry of Education. The *Consejo* consists of seven members who represent the following institutions: the *Universidad de El Salvador*, the oldest private university (i.e. the *Universidad Centroamericana*), two other private universities, a technical institution, the Ministry of Education, and the Ministry of Social and Economic Planning and Coordination.

Under the proposed law, the minimum requirements to establish a university can be paraphrased as follows: a) five majors must be offered, covering scientific, humanistic, and technical areas; b) regulations, study plans, course descriptions, and curricula must be submitted for approval by the *Consejo*; c) One research project must be programmed each year in each academic area; d) for degree programs, the faculty must hold the degree offered, and the institution must also have no fewer than two professors with a higher degree than that offered in each specialization; e) the institution must hire fulltime at least 25% of its faculty; f) an adequate physical infrastructure is needed, including library, laboratories, other research and recreational facilities.

The requirements for recognition as a Technical Institute echo those for the university, with the caveat that 50 percent of the faculty must be full time.

Institutional Profiles

Universidad Albert Einstein/UAE (Albert Einstein University)
Final Av. Albert Einstein
Urbanización Lomas de San Francisco
Calle Circunvalación No. 6, Block L
San Salvador
Tel: 73-3780, 3781, 3782

Established and authorized to award credentials: 1977

• **Enrollment:** 1447

Programs offered:	Credential:	Duration:
Business Administration	*licenciado*	5 years
Architecture	*arquitecto*	5 years
Environmental Design	*técnico*	5 years
Civil Engineering	*ingeniero*	5 years
Electrical Engineering	*ingeniero*	5 years
Industrial Engineering	*ingeniero*	5 years
Mechanical Engineering	*ingeniero*	5 years
Computer Engineering	*ingeniero*	5 years

Universidad Americana/UA (American University)

Established and authorized to award credentials: 1982
Inactive

Universidad Andrés Bello/UAB (Andres Bello University)
49a Av. Sur No. 737
San Salvador
Tel.: 23-8302

* **Enrollment:** (1991): 918

Universidad Autónoma de Santa Ana/*UNASA* (Autonomous University of Santa Ana)
9a Calle Poniente, / 6a y 8a Av. Sur #22
Santa Ana
Tel.: 41-0811, 47-7023, 41-1897
Fax: 41-2575, 47-7951

* **Enrollment** (1994): 764.

* **Organization:** *UNASA*, located in Santa Ana, offers nine programs of study. One-half of its 130 faculty members, who teach subjects ranging from medicine to special education, hold licentiate or medical degrees, while 49 others have master's degree level training.

    The university is housed in two buildings, with the following facilities: 21 classrooms, 2 libraries with a total of 1051 books and 535 magazines, 11 laboratories, a legal office, and a psychology clinic that is being established. The laboratories include 15 dental clinics, x-ray machines, a physical therapy clinic, and facilities for studying chemistry, physics, microbiology, anatomy, and other basic sciences. Other equipment includes two computers, six overhead projectors, and nine slide projectors.

Programs offered:	Credential:	Duration:
Medicine	*doctor*	7 years
Dental Surgery	*doctor*	6.5 years
Business Administration	*licenciado*	5 years
Social Work	*licenciado*	5 years
Psychology	*licenciado*	5 years
Special Education	*licenciado*	5 years
Legal Sciences	*licenciado*	5 years
Special Education	*profesorado*	3 years
Physical Therapy	*técnico*	3 years

Universidad Capitán General Gerardo Barrios/UGB
(Captain General Gerardo Barrios University)
4a Calle Poniente No. 207
San Miguel
Tel.: 61-0542

Centro Universitario de Usulután
9a Avenida Norte No. 5
Usulutan

Established and authorized to award credentials: June 11, 1982

* **Enrollment:** (1991): 1268

Programs offered	Credential	Duration
Business Administration	*licenciado*	5 years
Psychology	*licenciado*	5 years
Education	*licenciado*	5 years
Computer Science	*licenciado**	5 years
Education	*profesorado*	3 years
Social Sciences	*profesorado*	3 years
Mathematics and Physics	*profesorado*	3 years
Civil Engineering	*ingeniero*	5 years
Agricultural Engineering	*ingeniero*	5 years
Legal Sciences	*licenciado*	5 years

*(See Document 4.1)

Universidad Católica de Occidente/UNICO (Catholic University of the West)
1a Calle Poniente No. 32
Santa Ana
Tel.: 41-3217, 40-8785
Fax: 41-2655

Established in April 1982 and authorized to award credentials in July 1982.

- **Enrollment:** 1234

- **Faculty:** 88

- **Academic Year:** Two cycles, January to June and July to December.

- **Admission:** Completed application, secondary school diploma (*bachiller* or *maestro*), birth certificate.

- **Grading:** Scale of 1 to 10; minimum passing grade is 6.0; minimum cumulative grade point average to graduate is 7.0.

Programs offered:	Credential:	Duration:
Education	*licenciado*	5 years
Legal Sciences	*licenciado*	5 years
Business Administration Computer Science	*licenciado*	5 years
Agricultural Engineering (with specialization in Rural Development)	*ingeniero*	5 years
Industrial Engineering	*ingeniero*	5 years
Education with specialization in:		
Philosophy	*profesorado*	3 years
Special Education	*profesorado*	3 years
Social Sciences	*profesorado*	3 years
Commercial Sciences	*profesorado*	3 years
English	*profesorado*	3 years
Letters	*profesorado*	3 years
Mathematics and Physics	*profesorado*	3 years
Biology and Chemistry	*profesorado*	3 years
Business Administration Computer Science	*técnico*	3 years

Universidad Centroamericana "José Simeón Cañas"/UCA ("José Simeón Cañas" Central American University)
Autopista Sur, Final Avenida Rio Lempa
Jardines de Guadalupe

Antiguo Cuscaltán
San Salvador
Tel.: 24-0011

Established and authorized to award credentials: September 6, 1965

- **Enrollment:** 7500

- **Organization:** Ten classroom buildings, three laboratories with approximately 80 classrooms; engineering, architecture, and psychology laboratories. Four-story library containing 80,000 volumes. Athletics facilities include weight room, basketball, soccer, volleyball, and judo.

Programs offered:	Credential:	Duration
Business Administration	*licenciado*	5 years
Accounting	*licenciado*	6 years
Economics	*licenciado*	5 years
Sociology	*licenciado*	5 years
Legal Sciences	*licenciado*	5 years
Political Science	*licenciado*	5 years
Marketing	*técnico*	3 years
Financial Administration	*técnico*	3 years
Architecture	*arquitecto*	5 years
Civil Engineering	*ingeniero*	5 years
Industrial Engineering	*ingeniero*	5 years
Mechanical Engineering	*ingeniero*	5 years
Electrical Engineering	*ingeniero*	5 years
Chemical Engineering	*ingeniero*	5 years
Agricultural Engineering	*ingeniero*	5 years
Chemical Agricultural Engineering	*ingeniero*	5 years
Computer Sciences	*licenciado*	5 years
Philosophy	*licenciado*	5 years
Psychology	*licenciado*	5 years
Letters	*licenciado*	5 years
Social Sciences	*profesorado*	3 years
Philosophy	*profesorado*	3 years
Religious and Moral Sciences	*profesorado*	3 years.
Mathematics and Physics	*profesorado*	3 years
Biology and Chemistry	*profesorado*	3 years
Letters	*profesorado*	3 years

Universidad Cristiana de las Asambleas de Dios/UCAD
(Christian University of the Assemblies of God)
27a Calle Oriente No. 134
San Salvador
Tel.: 25-5046

Established and authorized to award credentials: September 21, 1983

- **Enrollment:** Approximately 900

Programs offered:	Credential:	Duration
Educational Administration	*licenciado*	5 years
Business Administration	*licenciado*	5 years
Accounting	*licenciado*	5 years
English Language	*licenciado*	5 years
Education	*licenciado*	5 years

Programs offered:	Credential:	Duration
Economics	*licenciado*	5 years
Theology, Missionary Studies	*licenciado*	5 years
Commercial Sciences	*profesorado*	3 years
Social Sciences	*profesorado*	3 years
Educational Administra.	*profesorado*	3 years
Philosophy	*profesorado*	3 years
Missionary Studies	*profesorado*	3 years
Mathematics and Physics	*profesorado*	3 years
Christian Education	*profesorado*	3 years
Letters	*profesorado*	3 years

***Universidad de Administración de Negocios/UNAN* (Business Administration University)**
Urb. Palomo Diagonal Universitaria No. 12
Alameda Roosevelt No. 2828
San Salvador
Tel.: 23-9727

Established and authorized to award credentials: September 16, 1988

- **Enrollment:** 141

Programs offered:	Credential:	Duration:
Economics	*licenciado*	5 years
Business Administration	*licenciado*	5 years
Accounting	*licenciado*	5 years
Marketing	*licenciado*	5 years
Public Relations and Advertising	*licenciado*	5 years
Computer Sciences	*técnico*	3 years
Business Administration	*técnico*	3 years
Marketing	*técnico*	3 years
Advertising	*técnico*	3 years
Public Relations	*técnico*	3 years
Executive Secretary	*técnico*	3 years
Administrator	*técnico*	3 years

***Universidad de Educación Integral/UNEI* (Integral Education University)**

Established and authorized to award credentials: December 19, 1984

- **Enrollment:** 258 (in 1991)

***Universidad de El Salvador/UES* (University of El Salvador)**
Ciudad Universitario
Final 25 Avenida Norte
San Salvador
Tel.: 25-8826, 25-8930, 25-6903, 25-9367

- **Enrollment:** Approximately 26,000

Established and authorized to award credentials: February 16, 1841. The *Universidad de El Salvador*, in addition to being the nation's premier center of higher education, has played an important and controversial role in Salvadoran politics. The military closed the university in 1972, again in 1976, and between 1980 and 1984. These problems were exacerbated after the university's reopening when an earthquake devastated much of the campus in 1986. In the last military conflict of 1989, an estimated $15 million in additional damage was incurred.

- **Organization:** The *Universidad de El Salvador* consists of eight colleges ("*facultades*"), each of which has its own building or buildings and library. All engineering programs have laboratory facilities, as do the programs in dentistry, medicine, agronomy, chemistry and pharmacy, and journalism. There is also a central library and athletic facilities.

    The newest branch of the *UES* is in San Miguelito. The university also has campuses in Santa Ana and San Miguel.

Programs offered:	Credential:	Duration:
Business Administration	*licenciado*	5 years
Accounting	*licenciado*	6 years
Economics	*licenciado*	5 years
Clinical Laboratory Technician	*licenciado*	5 years
Health Education	*licenciado*	5 years
Ecotechnology	*licenciado*	5 years
Dietician and Nutrition	*licenciado*	5 years
Nursing	*licenciado*	5 years
Physical Therapy	*técnico*	3 years
Library Sciences	*técnico*	3 years
Maternal-Infant Health	*técnico*	3 years
Anesthesiology	*técnico*	3 years
Radiotecnology	*técnico*	3 years
Architecture	*arquitecto*	5 years
Civil Engineering	*ingeniero*	5 years
Industrial Engineering	*ingeniero*	5 years
Mechanical Engineering	*ingeniero*	5 years
Electrical Engineering	*ingeniero*	5 years
Chemical Engineering	*ingeniero*	5 years
Agricultural Engineering	*ingeniero*	5 years
Plant Agronomy	*ingeniero*	5 years
Animal Science	*ingeniero*	5 years
Dental Surgery	*doctor**	5 years
Medicine	*doctor**	8 years
International Relations	*licenciado*	5 years
Sociology	*licenciado*	5 years
Legal Sciences	*licenciado*	5 years
Biology	*licenciado*	5 years
Philosophy	*licenciado*	5 years
Psychology	*licenciado*	5 years
Journalism	*licenciado*	5 years
English Language	*licenciado*	5 years
Education	*licenciado*	5 years
Fine Arts	*licenciado*	5 years
Mathematics	*licenciado*	5 years
Physics	*licenciado*	5 years
Food Sciences	*licenciado*	5 years
Chemistry and Pharmacy	*licenciado*	5 years
Chemistry	*licenciado*	5 years
Social Sciences	*profesorado*	3 years
Biology	*profesorado*	3 years
Chemistry	*profesorado*	3 years
Letters	*profesorado*	3 years
English	*profesorado*	3 years

* Medicine and dental surgery are first university degrees in El Salvador.

Universidad de la Paz **(Peace University)**

Established and authorized to award credentials: January 12, 1987. Inactive

Universidad del Vendedor Salvadoreño **(Salvadoran Sales University)**

Established and authorized to award credentials: December 19, 1984. Inactive

Universidad de Oriente/UNIVO **(University of the East)**
Avenida Gerardo Barrios No. 303
Contiguo a Camisería Norma
San Miguel
Tels.: 61-0964, 61-0542

Established and authorized to award credentials: June 25, 1982

- **Enrollment:** Approximately 2,000

- **Organization:** One building, library. Two plots of land for agronomy fieldwork.

Programs offered:	Credential:	Duration:
Business Administration	*licenciado*	5 years
Legal Sciences	*licenciado*	5 years
Education	*licenciado*	5 years
Psychology	*licenciado*	5 years
Sociology	*licenciado*	5 years
Agronomy	*ingeniero*	5 years
Civil Engineering	*ingeniero*	5 years
Mathematics and Physics	*profesorado*	3 years
Biology and Chemistry	*profesorado*	3 years
Social Sciences	*profesorado*	3 years
Letters	*profesorado*	3 years
Commercial Sciences	*profesorado*	3 years
Architecture	*arquitecto*	5 years

Universidad de Sonsonate/USO **(University of Sonsonante)**
2a Avenida Norte No. 6-6
Avenida Flavian Mucci, No. 5-11
Sonsonate
Tel.: 51-0674, 51-0866

Established and authorized to award credentials: July 26, 1982

- **Organization:** One building with 16 classrooms, science laboratory, and a basketball court.

Programs offered:	Credential:	Duration:
Economics	*licenciado*	5 years
Business Administration	*licenciado*	5 years
Public Accounting	*licenciado*	5 years
Psychology	*licenciado*	5 years
Education	*licenciado*	5 years
Legal Sciences	*licenciado*	5 years
Industrial Engineering	*ingeniero*	5 years
Electrical Engineering	*ingeniero*	5 years
Agricultural Engineering	*ingeniero*	5 years

Universidad Don Bosco/UDB (**Don Bosco University**)
Ciudadela Don Bosco
Calle Plan del Pino
Canton Venecia
Apartado Postal 1874
Soyapango
San Salvador
Tels.: 27-3459, 77-0163, 77-0162/5
Fax: 77-1399

Established and authorized to award credentials: March 8, 1984

- **Enrollment:** Approximately 1200

Programs offered:	Credential:	Duration:
Electronic Engineering	*ingeniero*	5 years
Telecommunications/Computer Science		
Industrial Electronics		
Electrical Engineering:	*ingeniero*	5 years
Electrical Energy Distribution Systems		
Electric Machines		
Transmission Systems		
Mechanical Engineering:	*ingeniero*	5 years
Metallurgy		
Machine Analysis		
Thermal and Fluid Systems		
Biomedical Engineering	*ingeniero*	5 years
Industrial Engineering	*ingeniero*	5 years
Computer Science	*ingeniero*	5 years
Education	*licenciado*	5 years
Communications	*licenciado*	5 years
Computer Science	*técnico*	3 years
Mechanics	*técnico*	3 years
Electricity	*técnico*	3 years
Electronics	*técnico*	3 years
Biomedical Technician	*técnico*	3 years
Pastoral Theology	*profesorado*	3 years

Universidad Evangélica de El Salvador/UEES (**Evangelical University of El Salvador**)
63 Av. Sur y Pasaje 1
No. 138 (por El Salvador del Mundo)
San Salvador
Tels. 98-3105, 98-3106, 23-6338, 23-6354

- **Enrollment:** Approximately 2623 (in 1991)

Established and authorized to award credentials: 1981. Classes are scheduled mornings, evenings, and weekends

Programs offered:	Credential:	Duration:
Medicine	*doctor*	8 years
Dietetics and Nutrition	*licenciado*	5 years
Dental Surgery	*doctor*	5 years
Agronomist with a focus on		
agricultural production	*ingeniero*	5 years
Special Education	*profesorado, licenciado*	3, 5 years
Preschool Education	*profesorado*	3 years

Programs offered:	Credential:	Duration
English Education	*profesorado*	3 years
Education	*licenciado*	5 years
English Translation and Interpretation	*licenciado*	5 years
University Administration and Teaching	*maestría*	Not reported
Human Resources Administration	*maestría*	Not reported
Supervision, Guidance, Human Development	*postgrado*	Not reported
Educational Administration	*postgrado*	Not reported

Also courses in theology and pastoral counseling.

***Universidad Francisco Gavidia/UFG* (Francisco Gavidia University)**
Alameda Roosevelt No. 3031
San Salvador
Tels: 24-5962/23-9704/24-2734
Fax: 24-2551

- **Enrollment:** 5321, 3600 fulltime (in 1994)

Established March 7, 1981 and authorized to award credentials: September 1983.

- **Organization:** The *Universidad Francisco Gavidia* has grown significantly since the original PIER Report on Central America. It is housed in seven buildings, which hold classrooms, administrative offices, laboratories, a library, and a computer center. The library has approximately 20,000 volumes, and the laboratories are equipped for biology, chemistry, mathematics, and language studies. Laboratory facilities include 40 microscopes and equipment for scientific research, 20 tape recorders and materials for language learning, and 35 personal computers. There is also an audiovisual department with slide projectors, videocassette recorders and cameras, musical instruments, and other electronic equipment.

  Fulltime studies require that the student be enrolled in courses of at least 20 credits per semester. Most popular majors include education (especially preschool level), marketing and advertising, business administration, teaching degrees in letters and social sciences, and computer science. Students are taught by 201 faculty members, 175 of whom teach part-time.

- **Grading:** 0.0 to 10.0; 6.0 is minimum passing grade. Students are required to have at least a 7.0 average to graduate. Between 1983 and 1993, the university awarded 3060 degrees.

Programs offered	Credential	Duration
College of Social Sciences		
Preschool Education	*licenciado*	5 years
Preschool Education	*profesorado*	3 years
Education	*licenciado*	5 years
Special Education	*licenciado*	5 years
Special Education	*profesorado*	3 years
Letters	*licenciado*	5 years
Letters	*profesorado*	3 years
Biology and Chemistry	*profesorado*	3 years
Psychology	*licenciado*	5 years
Mathematics, Physics	*profesorado*	3 years
Social Work	*licenciado*	5 years
English Language	*profesorado*	3 years
Adult Education	*icenciado*	5 years
Social Sciences	*profesorado*	3 years
Education, Mathematics and Physics	*licenciado*	5 years
Education, Biology, and Chemistry	*licenciado*	5 years
College of Legal Sciences		
Legal Sciences	*licenciado*	5 years

Programs offered	Credential	Duration
College of Economics		
Business Administration	*licenciado*	5 years
Public Accounting	*licenciado*	5 years
Marketing and Advertising	*licenciado*	5 years
Administrative Computer Systems	*licenciado*	5 years
Public Relations and Communications	*licenciado*	5 years
Commercialization	*técnico*	3 years
Public Relations	*técnico*	3 years
Accounting	*técnico*	3 years
International Commercialization	*técnico*	3 years
Commercial Sciences	*profesorado*	3 years
Computer Science	*profesorado*	3 years

Other programs include courses in: Educational Research and Evaluation, Computer Programming, and Typing.

Credentials Awarded: *Postgrado en Profesorado Universitario*, a postgraduate diploma in university teaching, and Master's Degrees in Educational Research and Evaluation, Pre-School Education, and Clinical Psychology.

Universidad Interamericana "Simón Bolívar"/UISB (**"Simon Bolívar" Inter-American University**)

Established and authorized to award credentials: March 27, 1990

Universidad José Matias Delgado/UJMD (**José Matias Delgado University**)
Km. 8 Calle a Santa Tecla
San Salvador
Tels.: 78-1272, 23-7336

Established and authorized to award credentials: December 14, 1977

• **Enrollment:** Approximately 3000

Programs offered:	Credential:	Duration:
Law	*licenciado*	5 years
Psychology	*licenciado*	5 years
Communication Sciences	*licenciado*	5 years
Philosophy	*licenciado*	5 years
Letters	*licenciado*	5 years
Economics	*licenciado*	5 years
Business Administration	*licenciado*	5 years
Marketing	*licenciado*	5 years
Agroindustry	*licenciado*	5 years
Computer Sciences	*licenciado*	5 years
Banking Administration	*licenciado*	5 years
Public Accounting	*licenciado*	5 years
Public Administration	*licenciado*	5 years
International Commercialization	*técnico*	not reported

Universidad Las Américas de El Salvador/ULAES (**The Americas University of El Salvador**)
3a, C. Ote. No. 111
San Salvador
Tel.: 22-2087

Established and authorized to award credentials: 1982

- **Enrollment:** Approximately 1500

Programs offered:	Credential:	Duration:
Economics	*licenciado*	5 years
Business Administration	*licenciado*	5 years
Public Accounting	*licenciado*	5 years
Public Administration	*licenciado*	5 years
International Relations	*licenciado*	5 years
Education Sciences	*licenciado*	5 years
Legal Sciences	*licenciado*	5 years
Customs Economics	*licenciado*	5 years
Psychology	*licenciado*	5 years
Industrial Engineering	*ingeniero*	5 years
Computation	*técnico*	3 years
Customs Economics	*técnico*	3 years
English	*técnico*	3 years
Commercial Sciences	*profesorado*	3 years
Education, Administration Option	*profesorado*	3 years

Universidad Leonardo Da Vinci/ULDV (Leonardo Da Vinci University)
Alameda Roosevelt No. 2139
San Salvador
Tel.: 23-6034

Established and authorized to award credentials: 1981

- **Enrollment:** Approximately 1,000

- **Organization:** One building, with laboratories and a library.

Programs offered:	Credential:	Duration:
Business Administration	*licenciado*	5 years
Public Relations and Publicity	*licenciado*	4.5 years*
Marketing	*licenciado*	4.5 years*
Business Administration	*técnico*	2.5 years*
Commercialization	*técnico*	3 years
Public Relations and Publicity	*técnico*	3 years

* According to the 1991 *Guía Universitaria Salvadoreña*

Universidad Luterana Salvadoreña/ULSA (Salvadoran Lutheran University)
Km. 3 Carretera a Planes de Renderos y
Autopista a Comalapa
San Salvador
Tel: 70-1470, 70-7002
Fax: 707222

Established and authorized to award credentials: December 6, 1988

- **Enrollment:** Approximately 100

- **Organization:** The *Universidad Luterana* consists of one building, a library, and a documentation center. Agroecology is described as a curriculum designed to train professionals in the applications of engineering, agronomy, and ecology for improved agricultural efficiency in the conservation, reproduction, and development of natural resources.

Programs offered	Credential	Duration
Social Work	*licenciado*	5 years
Economics	*licenciado*	5 years
Education	*licenciado*	5 years
Theology	*licenciado*	5 years
Social Work	*técnico*	3 years
Agroecology	*técnico*	3 years
Computer Science	*técnico*	3 years
Agroecology	*ingeniero*	5 years
Information Systems	*ingeniero*	5 years

***Universidad Manuel Luis Escamilla/UMLE* (Manuel Luis Escamilla University)**
1a C. Pte. 47a Av. Nte. No. 2514
San Salvador
Tel.: 23-0727

Established and authorized to award credentials: May 24, 1989

- **Enrollment:** Approximately 600

Programs offered:	Credential:	Duration:
Education Sciences	*licenciado*	5 years
Pre-school Education	*licenciado*	5 years
Business Administration	*licenciado*	5 years
Psychology	*licenciado*	5 years
Marketing and Publicity	*licenciado*	5 years
Computer Science	*licenciado*	5 years
Basic Education	*profesorado*	3 years
Special Education	*profesorado*	3 years
Preschool Education	*profesorado*	3 years
Commercial Sciences	*profesorado*	3 years
English	*profesorado*	3 years
Letters	*rofesorado*	3 years
Mathematics and Physics	*profesorado*	3 years
Biology and Chemistry	*profesorado*	3 years
Food Processing	*técnico*	3 years
Computation	*técnico*	3 years
Commercialization	*técnico*	3 years
Agroindustrial Business Administration	*técnico*	3 years

***Universidad Metropolitana de El Salvador/ UNIMET* (Metropolitan University of El Salvador)**
1a Avenida Norte y 5a Calle Poniente
San Salvador
Tel.: 21-0189

Established and authorized to award credentials: September 24, 1987

- **Enrollment:** Approximately 1200

Programs offered:	Credential:	Duration:
Social Work	*licenciado*	5 years
Public Accounting	*licenciado*	5 years
Business Administration	*licenciado*	5 years
Marketing	*licenciado*	5 years
English	*licenciado*	5 years

Programs offered:	Credential:	Duration:
Public Relations and Communications	*licenciado*	5 years
Educational Administration	*licenciado*	5 years
Educational Counseling	*licenciado*	5 years
Educational Supervision	*licenciado*	5 years
Letters	*profesorado*	3 years
Commercial Sciences	*profesorado*	3 years
English	*profesorado*	3 years
Social Sciences *	*profesorado*	3 years
Business Administration	*técnico*	3 years
Public Accounting	*técnico*	3 years
Marketing	*técnico*	3 years
Public Relations and Communications	*técnico*	3 years
Social Work	*técnico*	3 years
Systems Engineering and Computation	*ingeniero*	5 years

Universidad Militar **(Military University)**
Carretera Sta. Tecla
San Salvador
Tel.: 78-3144

Established as a state institution and authorized to award credentials on April 26, 1988.

Universidad Modular Abierta/ UMA **(Open Modular University)**

Established and authorized to award credentials: 1982.

- **Enrollment:** Approximately 5000 in 1991

Nine locations throughout El Salvador: (See Document 4.3)

3a Calle Poniente No. 1126
Nva. Concepción 3a Av. Sur
San Salvador

Contiguo Alcaldia Municipal
Tels. 22-9805, 22-3408, 22-3419
Chalatenango

Calle Libertad No. 13
Tel. 35-7019
Santa Ana

2a Calle Oriente No. 14
Tels. 41-3793, 41-2558
Usulutan

3a Calle Oriente No. 1-4
Tel. 62-0249
Ahuachapan

1a Calle Oriente No. 204
Tel: 43-1742
San Miguel

3a Ave. Nte. No. 5-1
Barrio El Pilar

5a Av. Nte No. 5 Frente Esc.
Tel. 61-2883
Sonsonate

Club de Leones
Tel. 51-1526

La Union
Tel. 64-4764

Avenida Juan Manuel Rodríguez
No. 38 Zacatecoluca
Tel. 34-0224

Note: UMA classes are generally held on weekends and evenings; most students study part-time.

- **Credentials Awarded:** 5.5-year _licenciado_ degrees in: Business Administration, Accounting, Legal Sciences, Psychology, Education, Letters, Preschool Education.
  3-year _técnico_ degrees in: Business Administration, Personnel Administration, Finance, Marketing.
  3-year _profesor_ degrees in: Education, Social Sciences, Special Education, English, Letters, Commercial Sciences, Preschool Education.

**Universidad Nueva San Salvador/UNSSA** **(New San Salvador University)**
Calle Arce y 23 Avenida Sur No. 1243
Apartado Postal 2596
San Salvador
Tel: 21-2288

Established and authorized to award credentials: 1981.

- **Enrollment:** Approximately 1360 (in 1991)

Programs offered:	Credential:	Duration:
	licenciado	5 years
	técnico	3 years
Advertising and Public Relations		
Social Work		
Marketing		
Education		
Financial Administration and Banking		5 years
Political Science		
Business Administration	_profesorado_	
Accounting		
Social Sciences		
Economics		
Financial Administration and Banking	_doctor_	
Law		
Dental Surgery		
Chemistry and Pharmacy		
Medicine and Surgery		7 years

Universidad Occidental de El Salvador (Western University of El Salvador)
6a Avenida Sur No. 52
Santa Ana
Tel.: 40-0224

Established July 14, 1981 and authorized to award credentials: August 30, 1981

- **Enrollment:** 427 (in 1994)

- **Organization:** The *Universidad Occidental* is a small private university housed in one building, which contains ten classrooms, a 2,000 volume library, two laboratories, and two computers for student use. It has 47 professors, 39 of whom hold a *licenciado* degree. There are 427 full time students (defined as students who are registered for at least 5 courses per semester.) The university's calendar runs in 2 semesters or "cycles", from April to August, and August to December. There is also an intensive cycle from January to March. Like most Salvadoran universities, the minimum passing grade is 6.0; the minimum grade point average required for graduation is 7.5. Approximately 173 degrees have been awarded since the institution's founding in 1981.

Credentials Awarded	Duration
licenciado	5 years
Business Administration	
Public Accounting	
Economics	
Psychology	
ingeniero	5 years
Agricultural Engineering	
Civil Engineering	
Electrical Engineering	
Industrial Engineering	
Mechanical Engineering	
técnico	3 years
Commercialization	
Computation	

Universidad Panamericana/UPA (Pan American University)

Established and authorized to award credentials: May 24, 1989

Universidad Pedagógica de El Salvador/UPES (Pedagogical University of El Salvador)
7a Avenida Norte No. 421
San Salvador
Tel.: 22-5052, 22-1614

Established and authorized to award credentials: 1982

- **Enrollment:** 678 (in 1991)

- **Organization:** The *UPES* offers the following programs in education. They operate on a daily and weekend schedule.

Programs offered:	Credential:	Duration:
Early Childhood Education	*licenciado*	5 years
Social Development Education	*licenciado*	5 years
Educational Administration	*licenciado*	5 years

Programs offered:	Credential:	Duration:
Education in:		
Philosophy and Letters	*licenciado*	5 years
Social Sciences	*licenciado*	5 years
Mathematics and Physics	*licenciado*	5 years
Biology and Chemistry	*licenciado*	5 years
Commercial Sciences	*licenciado*	5 years
Philosophy and Letters	*profesorado*	3 years
Biology and Chemistry	*profesorado*	3 years
Social Sciences	*profesorado*	3 years
Commercial Sciences	*profesorado*	3 years
Physics and Mathematics	*profesorado*	3 years
English	*profesorado*	3 years
Educational Administration	*técnico*	3 years
Social Development Educator	*técnico*	3 years
Educational Administration	*maestría*	not reported

Universidad Politécnica de El Salvador/UP (Polytechnic University of El Salvador)
17a Calle Poniente No. 233
San Salvador
Tel.: 21-1866

Established and authorized to award credentials: 1979

- **Enrollment:** 2,263

- **Organization:** Five buildings fitted with laboratories, computer center, and library.

Programs offered:	Credential:	Duration:
Economics	*licenciado*	5.5 years
Business Administration	*licenciado*	5.5. years
Public Accounting	*licenciado*	5.5. years
Marketing	*licenciado*	5.5 years
Architecture	*arquitecto*	5.5 years
Agronomist	*ingeniero*	5.5 years
Industrial Engineer	*ingeniero*	5.5 years
Civil Engineer	*ingeniero*	5.5 years
Electrical Engineer	*ingeniero*	5.5 years
Computer Science Engineer	*ingeniero*	5.5 years
Computation Systems	*técnico*	3 years
Commercialization Systems	*técnico*	3 years

Universidad Salvadoreña/USAL (Salvadoran University)
Edificio USAL av. Alvarado No. 164 y
Calle A San Antonio Abad
Col. Buenos Aires (Frente a Shell Centroamericana)
San Salvador
Tel. 25-3945, 25-8861
Fax. 25-8904

Established and authorized to award credentials: 1982. A private university specializing in computer sciences.

- **Enrollment:** 2,337

Programs offered	Credential	Duration
College of Economics		
Business Administration	*licenciado*	5 years
Accounting	*licenciado*	5 years
Marketing	*licenciado*	5 years
Commercialization	*técnico*	3 year
Executive Secretary with Computer option	*técnico*	3 years
College of Sciences and Humanities		
Psychology	*licenciado*	5 years
Communication Sciences	*licenciado*	5 years
Languages (English, French, German)	*licenciado*	5 years
Education	*licenciado*	5 years
Special Education	*profesorado*	3 years
Pre-school Education	*profesorado*	3 years
College of Engineering:		
Computer Systems Engineering	*licenciado*	5 years
Industrial Engineering	*licenciado*	5 years
Electrical Engineering	*licenciado*	5 years
Programming & Systems Analysis	*técnico*	3 years
College of Law		
Legal Sciences	*licenciado*	5 years
International Relations	*licenciado*	5 years
Political Science	*licenciado*	5 years

Universidad Salvadoreña "Alberto Masferrer"/USAM ("Alberto Masferrer" Salvadoran University)
Apartado Postal 2053
19 Av. Nte.
Entre 3a Calle Pte y Av. Juan Pablo II
San Salvador
Tels. 71-4601, 21-1136, 21-1137, 21-1138

Established and authorized to award credentials: 1980

- **Enrollment:** 1783 (in 1991)

Programs offered:	Credential:	Duration:
Medicine	*doctor**	7.5 years
Dental Surgery	*doctor**	5 years
Chemistry and Pharmacy	*licenciado*	5 years
Veterinary Medicine	*licenciado*	5.5 years
Jurisprudence and Social Sciences	*licenciado*	5.5 years

* Medicine and dental surgery are first university degrees in El Salvador.

Universidad Salvadoreña "Isaac Newton"/USIN ("Isaac Newton" Salvadoran University)
1a Avenida Norte No. 838
San Salvador
Tel.: 22-2131

Established and authorized to award credentials: 1982

- **Enrollment:** 246 in 1991

Programs offered:	Credential:	Duration:
Biology	*licenciado*	5 years
Psychology	*licenciado*	5 years
Letters	*licenciado*	5 years
Sociology	*licenciado*	5 years
Education Sciences	*licenciado*	5 years
Business Administration	*licenciado*	5 years
Public Accounting	*licenciado*	5 years
Mathematics	*licenciado*	5 years
Letters and Aesthetics	*profesorado*	3 years
Biology and Chemistry	*profesorado*	3 years
Social Sciences	*profesorado*	3 years
Commercial Sciences	*profesorado*	3 years
Physics and Mathematics	*profesorado*	3 years
Business Administration	*técnico*	3 years
Industrial Engineering	*ingeniero*	5 years

Universidad Santaneca de Ciencia y Tecnología/USCYT
(Santa Ana Science and Technology University)
9a Calle Poniente No. 1
Santa Ana
Tel.: 41-2399

Established and authorized to award credentials: December 12, 1982

- **Enrollment:** 114

- **Academic Year:** February to June, August to December

- **Organization:** A small institution in the city of Santa Ana, the *USCYT* has 114 students concentrating in 11 academic fields. Its most popular major is business administration (approximately half of the students concentrate in that area). *USCYT* is housed in one building, which contains 11 classrooms, a library with 100 volumes, 3 personal computers, and 10 drawing tables. The majority (35) of USCYT's 37 professors hold *licenciado* degrees.

- **Grading:** Grades range from 0 to 10; 6 is a passing grade and at least a 7 average is required for graduation.

Programs offered:	Degree	Duration:
Business Administration	*licenciado*	5 years
Public Accounting	*licenciado*	5 years
Economics	*licenciado*	5 years
Social Work	*licenciado*	5 years
Architecture	*licenciado*	5 years
Psychology	*licenciado*	5 years
Business Administration with a specialization in:		
Marketing	*técnico*	3 years
Personnel Administration	*técnico*	3 years
Accounting and Finance	*técnico*	3 years
Administrative Computation	*técnico*	3 years
English	*profesorado*	3 years

Universidad Técnica Latinoamericana/UTLA (Latin American Technical University)
4a Avenida Norte 2-5
Santa Tecla
San Salvador
Tel.: 28-1820, 28-0505, 28-4736

Established and authorized to award credentials: 1981

- **Enrollment:** Approximately 500

- **Facilities:** One building with 12 classrooms, electricity, electronics, and physics laboratories, and a library.

Programs offered:	Credential:	Duration:
Education	*licenciado*	5 years
Psychology	*licenciado*	5 years
Public Accounting	*licenciado*	5 years
Animal Husbandry	*licenciado*	5 years
Business Administration	*licenciado*	5 years
Agronomist	*ingeniero*	5 years
Civil Engineering	*ingeniero*	5 years
Electrical Engineering	*ingeniero*	5 years
Computer Engineering	*ingeniero*	5 years
Industrial Engineering	*ingeniero*	5 years
Mechanical Engineering	*ingeniero*	5 years
Programming Analyst	*técnico*	3 years
Computerized Accounting	*técnico*	3 years
Executive Secretary/Computers	*técnico*	3 years
Physics and Mathematics	*profesorado*	3 years
Biology and Chemistry	*profesorado*	3 years

Universidad Tecnológica/UTEC (Technological University)
Calle Arce No. 1020
San Salvador
Tel.: 71-4761

Established and authorized to award credentials: 1981

- **Faculty:** 275

- **Enrollment:** Approximately 9,800

- **Academic Year:** Two semesters; January to June and July to December.

Programs offered:	Credential:	Duration:
Legal Sciences	*licenciado*	5 years
Psychology	*licenciado*	5 years
Industrial Psychology	*licenciado*	5 years
English	*licenciado*	5 years
Business Administration	*licenciado*	5 years
Business Administration with Specialization in Computation	*licenciado*	5 years
Marketing	*licenciado*	5 years
Public Relations and Communications	*licenciado*	5 years
Public Accounting	*licenciado*	5 years

Programs offered:	Credential:	Duration:
Journalism	*técnico*	3 years
English	*profesorado*	3 years
Systems and Computer Engineering	*ingeniero*	5 years
Civil Engineering	*ingeniero*	5 years
Industrial Engineering	*ingeniero*	5 years
Finance Administration	*maestría*	2 years
Political Science and Public Administration	*maestría*	2 years
Business Administration	*maestría*	2 years
Diplomacy and International Relations	*maestría*	2 years
Education	*maestría*	2 years

Universidad Tomás Alva Edison/UTAE (Tomás Alva Edison University)
23a Calle Poniente y Avenida Las Victorias
No. 1
San Salvador
Tel.: 25-4207

Established and authorized to award credentials : 1985

• **Enrollment:** Approximately 300

Programs offered:	Credential:	Duration:
Business Administration	*licenciado*	5.5 years
Public Accounting	*licenciado*	5.5 years
Marketing	*licenciado*	5.5 years
Industrial Engineering	*ingeniero*	5.5 years
Electronic Engineering	*ingeniero*	5.5 years
Systems Engineering	*ingeniero*	5.5 years

Technical Education: *Institutos de Educación Tecnológica*

According to the Ministry of Education's statistics on higher education (*Educación superior en cifras, 1991-1992*), the following are recognized institutions that grant postsecondary *técnico* degrees. As the statistics indicate, enrollment in both public and private technical institutes dropped significantly between 1987 and 1991.

Table 4.1 Public Institutions

Name:	Number of Students (1987)	Number of Students (1991)
Instituto Tecnológico Centroamericano	1,566	1,035
Instituto Tecnológico Gral. Francisco Menéndez	408 (Became part of Instituto Tec. Centroamericano, 1988)	
Instituto Tecnológico Metropolitano	*	298
Instituto Tecnológico de Zacatecoluca	297	154
Instituto Tecnológico de San Vicente	384	169
Instituto Tecnológico de Usulutan	408	163
Instituto Tecnológico de San Miguel	431	238
Instituto Tecnológico de Chalatenango	254	114
Instituto Tecnológico de Santa Ana	739	435
Instituto Tecnológico de Sonsonate	359	333
Escuela Superior de Educación Física y Deporte	122	113
Escuela Nacional de Agricultura	250	205
Escuela Superior de Música	*	*

(continued-) Name:	Number of Students (1987)	Number of Students (1991)
Escuela Nacional de Enfermería	28	*
Escuela de Trabajo Social de El Salvador	*	*
Escuela Militar	*	*
Total	5,246	3,257

* Information not reported

Table 4.2 Private Institutions

Name:	Number of Students (1987)	Number of Students (1991)
Instituto Tecnológico "Salarrue"	110	36
Colegio Tecnológico "Espirtu Santo"	320	37
Instituto Tecnológico "La Salle"	92	
Instituto Tecnológico El Salvador	54	
Escuela Superior de Enfermería "Florence Nightingale"	194	161
Centro Internacional de Programación de Computos	740	
Instituto Superior de Tecnología y Administración	55	14
Instituto Superior de Venta Púb. y Mercadeo	248	
Centro Técnico de Capacitación Contable	145	195
Liceo Tecnológico "Dr. Manuel Luis Escamilla"	150	65
Instituto Tecnológico Las Américas		
Colegio Tecnológico "Ana Guerra de Jesús"		
Centro de Capacitación Bancaria		164
Total	2,703	1,084

\- Information not listed

Glossary

Abogado(a). Lawyer

Aprobado(a). Passed

Arquitecto(a). Architect

Bachillerato or _bachiller_. First university degree in some countries; generally translated as secondary school diploma.

Bachiller Mayor. Two-year university-level degree

Bibliotecario. Librarian

Carrera. Program of study/major/specialization

Cirujano Dentista. Dental Surgeon

Doctor(a)/Doctorado. Doctor, usually of medicine or dentistry (a first university degree in Central America); also may be a graduate level doctorate in philosophy, a credential recognized under the proposed Education Law

Enfermero(a)/Enfermería. Nurse/Nursing

Especialización. Specialization

Ingeniero(a)/Ingeniería. Engineer(ing)

Licenciado(a)/Licenciatura. Licentiate, generally first university degree

Maestría. Master's

Maestro/a. Teacher

Médico(a)/Medicina. Medical Doctor/Medicine

Odontología. Dentistry

Pensum. List of required courses and prerequisites for a specific program; also called _plan de estudios_ (study plan)

Perito. Expert

Profesorado. Teaching degree

Profesorado. Universitario Postgraduate diploma in university teaching

Profesor(a) en (specialization). Teacher of (specialization)

Reprobado(a). Failed

Técnico. Technician

Técnico avanzado. Advanced Technician

Título. Title/ degree

Unidades Valorativas (u.v.). Credits, i.e.; "value units"

UNIVERSIDAD "CAPITAN GENERAL GERARDO BARRIOS"

4a. Calle Poniente No. 209, San Miguel. Teléfono: 61-2947
Centro Universitario de Usulután, Carretera El Litoral Km. 113.
Teléfono: 62-0846.

EL INFRASCRITO ADMINISTRADOR ACADEMICO DE LA UNIVERSIDAD CAPITAN GENERAL " GERARDO BARRIOS "

HACE CONSTAR QUE: La Bachiller ...., con código NQ .... (....), ha cursado en esta Universidad, las asignaturas abajo detalladas en la carrera de **LICENCIATURA EN COMPUTACION.** Sample Document

CICLO I AÑO ACADEMICO 1991.

MATEMATICAS I.	8.3 (Ocho punto tres)	APROBADA.
CONTABILIDAD I.	8.3 (Ocho punto tres)	APROBADA.
PSICOLOGIA GENERAL.	7.6 (Siete punto seis)	APROBADA.
SOCIOLOGIA GENERAL.	8.1 (Ocho punto uno)	APROBADA.

CICLO II AÑO ACADEMICO 1991.

MATEMATICAS II.	8.4 (Ocho punto cuatro)	APROBADA.
CONTABILIDAD II.	6.5 (Seis punto cinco)	APROBADA.
PRINCIPIOS GRALES. DE ECONOMIA.	8.8 (Ocho punto ocho)	APROBADA.
TEORIA ADMINISTRATIVA I.	8.7 (Ocho punto siete)	APROBADA.

INTER-CICLO AÑO ACADEMICO 1991.

INGLES I.	9.4 (Nueve punto cuatro)	APROBADA.

CICLO I AÑO ACADEMICO 1992.

ESTADISTICA I.	8.2 (Ocho punto dos)	APROBADA.
CONTABILIDAD DE COSTOS I.	7.6 (Siete punto seis)	APROBADA.
TEORIA ADMINISTRATIVA II.	8.5 (Ocho punto cinco)	APROBADA.
COMPUTACION.	8.7 (Ocho punto siete)	APROBADA.

PASAN...

HACIA UNA FORMACION PROFESIONAL, HUMANA, RESPONSABLE Y ACTUALIZADA

Document 4.1 Partial transcript for a *licenciado* program in computer science at the *Universidad "Capítan General Gerardo Barrios."*

UNIVERSIDAD "CAPITAN GENERAL GERARDO BARRIOS"

4a. Calle Poniente No. 209, San Miguel. Teléfono: 61-2947
Centro Universitario de Usulután, Carretera El Litoral Km. 113.
Teléfono: 62-0846.

...VIENEN.

Sample Document

CICLO II AÑO ACADEMICO 1992.

ESTADISTICA II.	9.1 (Nueve punto uno)	APROBADA.
CONTABILIDAD DE COSTOS II.	8.8 (Ocho punto ocho)	APROBADA.
INGLES II.	8.9 (Ocho punto nueve0	APROBADA.
PROGRAMACION ESTRUCTURADA.	8.1 (Ocho punto uno)	APROBADA.
LEGISLACION APLIC.A LA EMPRESA.	8.2 (Ocho punto dos)	APROBADA.

CICLO I AÑO ACADEMICO 1993.

INTRODUCCION AL MERCADEO.	7.0 (Siete punto cero)	APROBADA.
MATEMATICAS FINANCIERA.	9.0 (Nueve punto cero)	APROBADA.
ESTRUCTURA DE DATOS.	8.6 (Ocho punto seis)	APROBADA.
DISEÑO DE APLICACIONES.	7.6 (Siete punto seis)	APROBADA.
PROGRAMACION I	8.3 (Ocho punto tres)	APROBADA.

CICLO II AÑO ACADEMICO 1993.

INVESTIGACION OPERATIVA.	6.9.(Seis punto nueve)	APROBADA.
ADMINISTRACION FINANCIERA.	7.2 (Siete punto dos)	APROBADA.
SISTEMAS OPERATIVOS.	7.9 (Siete punto nueve)	APROBADA.
ANALISIS DE SISTEMAS.	7.8 (Siete punto ocho)	APROBADA.
PROGRAMACION II.	8.0 (Ocho punto cero)	APROBADA.

ESCALA DE CALIFICACION: De cero punto cero (0.0) a diez punto cero (10.0).

NOTA MINIMA DE APROBAR: Es seis punto cero (6.0). Esta constancia

PASAN...

HACIA UNA FORMACION PROFESIONAL, HUMANA, RESPONSABLE Y ACTUALIZADA

Document 4.1.2 (see previous)

UNIVERSIDAD "CAPITAN GENERAL GERARDO BARRIOS"

4a. Calle Poniente No. 209, San Miguel. Teléfono: 61-2947
Centro Universitario de Usulután, Carretera El Litoral Km. 113.
Teléfono: 62-0846.

...VIENEN.

ampara veintiocho (28) asignaturas aprobadas.

Sample Document

Y para los usos que la interesada estime convenientes, se extiende, firma y sella la presente, en la Ciudad de San Miguel, a veintitrés días del mes de mayo de mil novecientos noventa y cuatro.

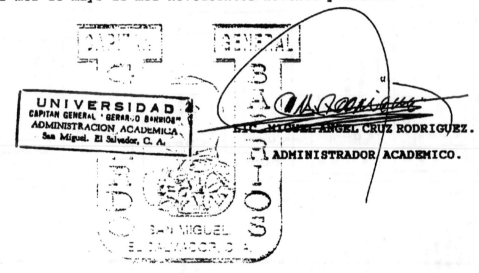

LIC. MIGUEL ANGEL CRUZ RODRIGUEZ.

ADMINISTRADOR ACADEMICO.

ELABORO Y CONFRONTO: ANA FRANCISCA GARCIA PEÑA.

HACIA UNA FORMACION PROFESIONAL, HUMANA, RESPONSABLE Y ACTUALIZADA

Document 4.1.3 (see previous)

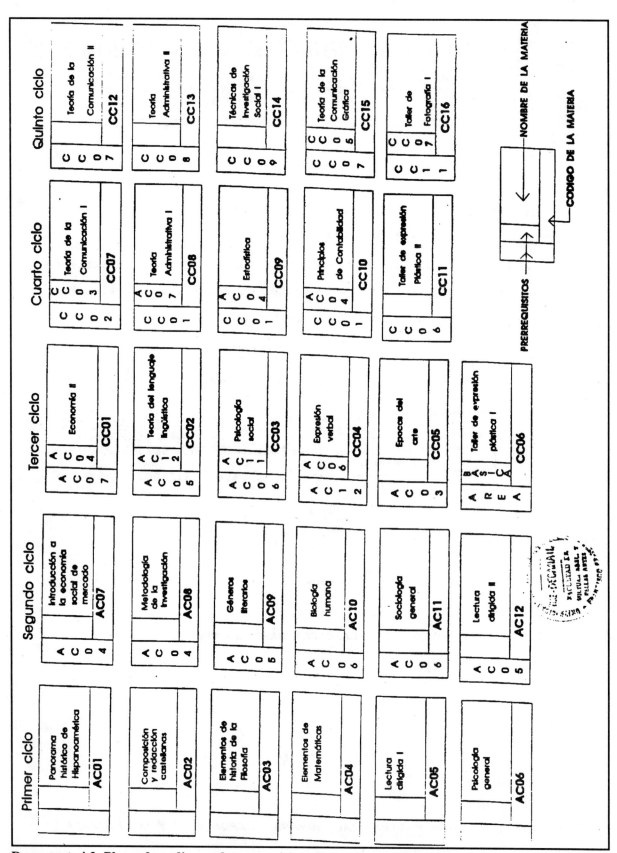

Document 4.2 Plan of studies and prerequisites for a 5-year degree in Communications.

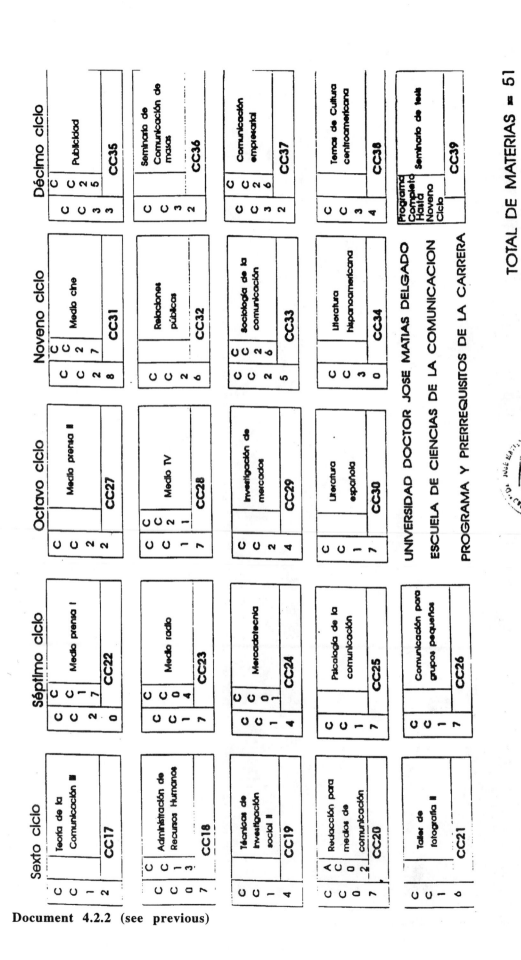

UNIVERSIDAD DOCTOR JOSE MATIAS DELGADO

ESCUELA DE CIENCIAS DE LA COMUNICACION

PROGRAMA Y PRERREQUISITOS DE LA CARRERA

TOTAL DE MATERIAS = 51

Document 4.2.2 (see previous)

Document 4.3 Map of El Salvador showing the branch locations of the Universidad Modular Abierta

Chapter 5
The Educational System of Guatemala

The Country

Guatemala is a nation rich with tradition and a rainbow of indigenous languages, peoples, and colors. It has had a turbulent political history, both as the original site of the vast Mayan civilization that dominated the region before the Spanish conquest, and later when it was the seat of colonial rule for all of Central America. Guatemala is bordered on the north and west by Mexico, on the east by Belize, and on the southeast are El Salvador and Honduras.

As a result of both economic and political hardship, numerous Guatemalans have emigrated to Mexico and other neighboring countries over the years. Gaining access to education, health facilities, and potable water are problems that continue to make life difficult for much of Guatemala's population. Despite these obstacles, there is currently underway in the universities an effort to "recapture" the country's linguistic and cultural traditions. Government programs teach inhabi-

tants to speak and write their native languages, and many newly launched anthropological and archeological investigations are increasing in Guatemala.

Postsecondary Education

Of the seven Central American nations examined in this report, Guatemalan higher education has changed the least. As reported in the 1987 PIER Workshop Report (*The Admission and Placement of Students from Central America*), postsecondary education in Guatemala is offered at one public university and four private universities. The state university, *San Carlos de Guatemala/USAC*, is the oldest university in Central America. Despite political activities that have caused some degree of disruption during the past decade, the 300-year-old *USAC* is a stable institution that is well supported by the Guatemalan government. The private universities, all of which have been established since the 1960s, are also well equipped and offer students a variety of academic options.

Official name: Republic of Guatemala

Area: 108,780 square kilometers/42,000 square miles (about the size of Tennessee)

Capital: Guatemala City

Population: 9 million

Annual growth rate: 3 percent

Noun and adjective: Guatemalan(s)

Ethnic groups: Mestizos, numerous indigenous groups

Languages: Spanish, 23 indigenous languages mainly belonging to four groups: Quiché, Mam, Cakchiquel, Kekchi

Religion: Catholic, Protestant minority, traditional Mayan

Education: Years compulsory-6; Attendance-35%; Literacy-52%

(Source: U.S. State Department *Background Notes*)

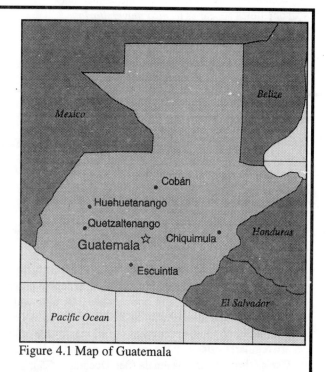

Figure 4.1 Map of Guatemala

There are numerous professional institutes (*institutos profesionales*) offering non-university training programs at the postsecondary level. Some of these are schools of nursing, a military academy, and a school for the training of occupational and physical therapists. These programs are authorized by the ministry with which they are affiliated. For example, the schools of nursing and physical therapy are administered by the Ministry of Public Health and Social Welfare. For a complete listing of these institutes, please refer to the original PIER Workshop Report on Central America.

Despite the variety of options available, only about 6 percent of the eligible age group in Guatemala participate in postsecondary education (*World Education News & Reviews*, Vol. 7, No. 1, Winter 1993).

Private universities receive authorization to operate through the Council of Private Higher Education (*Consejo de Educación Superior Privado*). As of the mid-1980s, this council consisted of two representatives from USAC, two representatives from the private universities, and one from the private institutes or associations.

Academic credentials and titles

In Guatemala, as in other Central American countries, a person who successfully completes a program of study (*carrera*) and all other degree requirements, is usually awarded a field-specific title (*título*) that designates the academic level (*grado académico*) of the program completed.

- At the intermediate level: *profesorado* (teacher), *diplomado* (diploma holder), and *técnico* (technician) are awarded. The title *técnico* may sometimes appear as *técnico universitario* (university-level technician) to distinguish it from *técnicos* at the secondary level. Intermediate degree programs in Guatemala are 2 to 3.5 years in length, except for three 4-year

profesorado programs offered by the *Universidad Mariano Galvez*. Intermediate programs are structured either as short programs of study (*carreras cortas*) or intermediate programs of study (*carreras intermedias*). These degrees are awarded by the universities and also by non-university postsecondary institutions in Guatemala.

- At the first degree level: *licenciado*. These programs are 4 to 6 years in length and usually require a thesis.

- At the graduate (*postgrado*) level: *maestría* and *doctor*.

Duration of *Carreras*

As the 1987 PIER Report states, students are required to complete all courses of a *carrera* to earn a degree. Most academic programs are designed to prepare the student for a particular program, and as such are quite specialized. The plan of study defines which courses are to be taken, and there are generally few electives. A fulltime load of courses varies depending on the program and the faculty, and where "duration" is cited in institutional profiles, it refers to the standard length of the program when pursued fulltime. Students frequently take much longer to complete a degree program, as many of them work and attend school part-time.

Guatemalan institutions recognize that many of their students work and study simultaneously, and their schedules reflect this reality. Many programs are offered on morning (*matutina*), afternoon (*vespertina*), evening (*nocturna*), and Saturday (*sabatina*) schedules.

Institutional Profiles

Universidad San Carlos de Guatemala/USAC (San Carlos University of Guatemala)
Ciudad Universitaria
Zona 12
Guatemala
Tel.: 760790, 760985/86/88

- **Enrollment:** Approximately 55,000

- **Organization:** Classes are offered in several shifts, and students can attend morning, afternoon, evening, or Saturday programs. There are also several degree programs that are offered all day (e.g. medicine and dentistry). Morning classes generally run between 7:00 a.m. and 1:00 p.m. Afternoon classes begin at approximately 2:00 p.m. and end at about 9:00 p.m. Evening schedules begin at 5 p.m. (after work) and also end at approximately 9 p.m. It is important to note that not all majors are offered at all locations in each of these shifts. However, most are regularly offered at the main campus in Guatemala City every year. Regional centers of the *Universidad San Carlos* throughout Guatemala (See Document 5.1):

Centro de Aprendizaje de Lenguas de la Universidad de San Carlos de Guatemala/CALUSAC
Escuela de Formación de Profesores de Ensenanza Media/EFPEM
Centro de Estudios del Mar y Acuicultura/CEMA, Monterrico
Centro Universitario de Occidente/CUNOC, Quezaltenango
Centro Universitario del Norte, Alta Verapaz/CUNOR, Cobán
Centro Universitario del Oriente/CUNORI, Chiquimula
Centro Universitario del Nor Occidente/CUNOROC, Huehuetenango
Centro Universitario del Sur/CUNSUR, Esquintla
Centro Universitario del Sur Occidente/CUNSUROC, Mazatenango, Suchitepequez
Centro Universitario del Sur Oriente/CUNSURORI, Jalapa

Branch campuses are designated by the city in which they are located: Capital (Guatemala City), Antigua Guatemala, Chimaltenango, Jutiapa, Retalhuleu, Chiquimula, Sololá, Quiché, Jalapa, Coatepeque, Barberena, Panzos, Tactic, El Petén, Salama, Jacaltenango, Ipala, Poptún (Petén), El Estor (Izabal).

The university is divided into three large areas of study: social humanistic, scientific technology, and scientific assistance. All majors fall into these categories, which can be characterized as relating to human relations, knowledge and modification of the physical environment, and health issues, respectively. Each of the three areas is divided into a study sector, into which specific majors are grouped.

The degrees listed in the most recent course catalog at the San Carlos are: *técnico, profesorado, licenciado, and maestría* in the areas that follow. In the social sciences a 3-year "short degree" (*carrera corta*) is also offered. Programs offered in the social humanistic area (i.e. social sciences and humanities), are divided into study sectors.

Social Humanistic

Program offered	Credential	Duration
Education and Teacher Training Majors	(*Carreras*):	
Pedagogy	*licenciado*	5 years
Pedagogy	*profesorado*	3.5 years
Mathematics	*profesorado*	3.5 years
Biology	*profesorado*	3.5 years
Physics	*profesorado*	3.5 years
Chemistry	*profesorado*	3.5 years
Physics/Math	*profesorado*	4 years
Chemistry/Biology	*profesorado*	4 years
Economics/Accounting Science	*profesorado*	3.5 years
History/SocialSciences	*profesorado**	3.5 years
Psychology	*profesorado*-*	3 years
Languages/Literature	*profesorado*-*	3.5 years
Philosophy	*profesorado*-*	3.5 years
English**	*profesorado*	3.5 years
Fine Arts/Art History	*profesorado*-*	3 years
Music Education	*profesorado*	3 years
Special Education	*profesorado**	3 years
Graphic Design	*técnico*	3 years

* A *licenciado* may be earned in these areas with 2 additional years of study.
** Students must pass an English proficiency examination to be admitted to this program.

Program offered	Credential	Duration
__Fine and Applied Arts Majors__	(*carreras*)	
Art	*licenciado*	5 years
Fine Furniture Restoration**	*técnico**	2 years
Museum Studies	*técnico**	2 years
Graphic Design for Education	*técnico**	2 years

NOTE: 4 hours of practical training each Saturday are required for these programs.
* A *licenciado* degree may be earned in these areas with 3 additional years of study.
**Only 10 students per year are admitted to this program.

__Humanities Majors (*carreras*)__

Languages and Literature	*licenciado*	5 years
History	*licenciado*	5 years
Archeology	*licenciado*	5 years
Philosophy	*licenciado*	5 years
Modern Languages*	*licenciado*	Special Schedule

* Includes studies in German, French, English, Italian, Portuguese, Quiché, and Cakchiquel

__Social Sciences and Behavior Majors__ (*carreras*)

Economics	*licenciado*	5 years
Political Science	*licenciado*	5 years
Sociology	*licenciado*	5 years
Anthropology	*licenciado*	5 years
Psychology	*licenciado*	5 years

__Business Administration and Related Fields Majors__ (*carreras*)

Business Administration	*licenciado*	5 years
Business Administration	*técnico*	3 years
Public Accounting and Auditing	*licenciado*	5 years

__Law Majors__ (*carreras*) See Document 5.1

Legal and Social Sciences	*licenciado*	5 years
Attorney and Notary	*licenciado*	5 years
International Relations	*licenciado*	5 years

__Documentation and Social Communication Majors__ (*carreras*)

Professional Journalist	*técnico*	3 years
Professional Broadcaster	*técnico*	3 years
Professional Publicist	*técnico*	3 years
Communication Sciences	*licenciado*	5 years
Library Assistant	*técnico*	2 years
General Librarian	*técnico**	3 years
Library Sciences	*licenciado*	5 years

* A *licenciado* degree in Library Sciences can be obtained with two additional years of study

__Other Programs in the Social Humanistic Area Majors__ (*carreras*):

Social Work	*trabajador social*	3 years
Social Work	*licenciado*	5 years
Professional Counseling	*técnico*	3 years
Speech Therapy	*técnico*	3 years
Occupational Therapy	*técnico*	3 years

Scientific Technology

Programs offered in the scientific technology area (i.e. programs related to the knowledge and modification of the physical environment), are divided into the following study sectors:

Program offered	Credential	Duration
Mathematics and Computer Science Majors	(*carreras*)	
Applied Mathematics	*licenciado*	5 years
Sciences and Systems	*licenciado*	5 years
Engineering and Technology Majors	(*carreras*)	
Chemical Engineering	*licenciado*	5 years
Civil Engineering	*licenciado*	5 years
Electrical Engineering	*licenciado*	5 years
Industrial Engineering	*licenciado*	5 years
Mechanical Engineering	*licenciado*	5 years
Mechanical/Industrial Engineering	*licenciado*	6 years
Mechanical/Electrical Engineering	*licenciado*	6 years

NOTE: Offered as a 5-year *licenciado* program in Quetzaltenango only.

Architecture and Urban Studies Majors	(*carreras*)	
Architecture	*licenciado*	5 years

* Offered only at Guatemala City campus

Agricultural Teaching Majors	(*carreras*)	
Renewable Resources Agronomy	*licenciado*	5 years
Agronomist in Agricultural Production Systems	*licenciado*	5 years
Forestry, Forest Management	*técnico*	3 years
Forestry Engineering	*licenciado*	5 years
Conservation and Management of Tropical Forests	*técnico*	3 years
Agricultural Production	*técnico*	3 years
Tropical Agronomy	*licenciado*	5 years
Fruit Production	*técnico*	3 years
Agronomy	*licenciado*	5 years
Agriculture with concentration in non-traditional crops	*licenciado*	5 years
Agroindustrial Processes	*técnico*	3 years
Agroindustries	*licenciado*	5 years

Animal (Cattle) Science Majors	(*carreras*)	
Veterinary Medicine	*licenciado*	6 years
Animal Science	*licenciado*	5 years
Cattle Production	*técnico*	3 years
Agriculture/Animal Production	*técnico*	3 years

Scientific Assistance

Programs offered in the scientific assistance area (i.e. programs related to health and the natural sciences), are divided into the following study sectors:

Natural Sciences Majors	(*carreras*):	
Biology	*licenciado*	5.5 years
Aquaculture	*técnico*	3.5 years

Program offered	Credential	Duration
Chemistry	*licenciado*	5 years
Physics	*licenciado*	5 years
Geology	*técnico*	3 years
Geology	*licenciado*	5 years

Medical Sciences Majors	(*carreras*)	
Medicine and Surgery	*licenciado*	6 years
Dentistry	*licenciado*	6 years
Pharmaceutical Chemistry	*licenciado*	5 years
Chemistry/Biology	*licenciado*	5 years

Food and Nutrition Majors	(*carreras*)	
Nutrition	*licenciado*	5 years
Vegetable Food Processing	*técnico*	3 years
Food Engineering	*licenciado*	5 years

Universidad Del Valle de Guatemala (Del Valle University of Guatemala)
18 Av. 11-95
Zona 15
Vista Hermosa III
Apartado no. 82
Guatemala City
Tel: 692563, 692776, 692827

Established in 1966, the *Universidad Del Valle* emerged from the American School of Guatemala in Guatemala City. It was authorized to function as a separate and independent entity by the *Universidad Nacional de San Carlos*. Until 1976, the university operated in the afternoons and evenings, using the American School's facilities. Construction of its library and laboratory, which are located on the same campus as the American School, was completed in 1977. Since the original construction began, over $11 million has been invested in the institution's infrastructure. Many of these funds have come from a series of grants from the Office of American Schools and Hospitals Abroad of the U.S. Agency for International Development. The campus today consists of science laboratories, a 50,000 volume library, classrooms, a computer lab with 150 personal computers, and administrative offices.

- **Academic Year:** University College, Faculties of Sciences and Humanities and Social Sciences; First semester: January-May (17 weeks); Summer session: June-July (8 weeks); Second semester: August-December (17 weeks). Faculty of Education; First semester: January-July (20 weeks); Second semester: July-December (20 weeks).

- **Enrollment:** Approximately 1,000 full/750 part-time

- **Credentials Awarded:** The *Universidad Del Valle* grants the following degrees: *profesorado*, *baccalaureatus*, *licenciado*, and *maestría*. The *profesorado* degrees, including the *profesor de enseñanza media* (elementary education) or *profesor de educación especial* (special education), require 3 or 4 years of study, which generally takes place on a weekend schedule.

  The university also awards 3-year *baccalaureatus* degrees, which it calls a B.A. or B.S., depending upon the course of study. These degrees may be obtained after passing, with a minimum grade point average of 70, the first 3 years of *licenciado* courses in the Faculties of Sciences and Humanities, and Social Sciences. This option is available in all academic areas except the programs in Letters and History.

  Students in the Faculty of Education and in the areas of Letters and History can earn a *baccalaureatus* after passing the general courses required in the *licenciado* program in the Social Sciences, plus the courses necessary to complete a minimum of 120 credits.

Those students who wish to obtain a *baccalaureatus* degree without enrolling in a *licenciado* program may enroll in the *baccalaureatus* program of the University College (*Colegio Universitario*). This program requires students to pass general education courses in humanities, social sciences, natural sciences, and mathematics, and other courses in their area of interest, for the minimum 120 credits.

The *Del Valle* describes the difference between the *baccalaureatus* and *licenciado* degrees as follows: the *baccalaureatus* is an academic degree, not a professional degree. Students with the former degrees may, however, continue in the professional programs. *Baccalaureatus* holders may opt for a *profesorado* degree, for example, by completing five courses in the Education Faculty and carrying out supervised teaching training practica.

The *licenciado* programs are 5 years in length at the *Universidad Del Valle*. In general, the first 3 years of the 5-year programs are made up of disciplinary, general education courses, and the last 2 years provide the training and skills needed in professional practice. A senior thesis or research project is required of all candidates for the *licenciado* degree. There are also master's degree programs (*maestría*), which vary based upon student demand and faculty availability. They consist of 1 or 2 years of study beyond the *licenciado*.

University College (*Colegio Universitario*) : baccalaureatus in artibus, baccalaureatus in scientiis

Program offered	Credential
Science and Humanities	
Biology	*licenciado*
Biochemistry	*licenciado*
Chemistry	*licenciado*
Physics	*licenciado*
Physics and Chemistry	*licenciado*
Mathematics	*licenciado*
Agriculture	*licenciado*
Food Science	*licenciado*
Nutrition	*licenciado*
Computer Science	*licenciado*
Engineering	*licenciado*
Civil Engineering	*licenciado*
Electronic Engineering	*licenciado*
Industrial Engineering	*licenciado*
Mechanical Engineering	*licenciado*
Chemical Engineering	*licenciado*
Structural Engineering	*maestría*
Pharmaceutical Chemistry	*licenciado*
Environmental Studies	*licenciado*
Earth Science	*licenciado*
Ecotourism	*licenciado*
Forest Science	*licenciado*
Letters	*licenciado*
Music	*licenciado*
Social Sciences	
Anthropology	*licenciado*
Archaeology	*licenciado*
History	*licenciado*
Psychology	*licenciado*
Education	
Special Education	*profesorado*
Learning Problems	*profesorado*
Education for children with hearing problems	*profesorado*

Program offered	Credential
Elementary Education with emphasis in:	
Biology and Chemistry	*profesorado en enseñanza media*
History and Social Sciences	*profesorado en enseñanza media*
Language and Literature	*profesorado en enseñanza media*
Mathematics and Physics	*profesorado en enseñanza media*
Mathematics and Computation	*profesorado en enseñanza media*
Population and Environmental Sciences	*profesorado en enseñanza media*
Education	*licenciado*
Education with specialization in:	
Educational Administration	*maestría*
Curriculum development	*maestría*
Measurement, Research, and Evaluation	*maestría*
Health Education	*licenciado*

Universidad Francisco Marroquín/UFM (Francisco Marroquín University)
6a Avenida 0-28, Zona 10
Guatemala City
Tel.: 34-68-86 to 95

- Academic Year: Two semesters, January to June and July to November.

- Grading: Grades range from 0 to 100, with 61 the minimum passing grade. Each class is assigned a number of credits (*Unidades de Mérito Académico* or *UMAs*), with each credit equivalent to 18 class periods. The *técnico* in social communication is a prerequisite for the *licenciado* degree. *Licenciado* degrees require a general examination and a written thesis for graduation.

Program offered	Credential	Duration
Journalism	*licenciado*	5 years
Publicity	*liceñciado*	5 years
Social Communication Sciences	*técnico*	3 years
Social Communications Sciences	*profesorado*	4 years
Social Communications Sciences	*licenciado*	6 years
Systems Information Administration	*licenciado*	5 years

Universidad Mariano Galvez de Guatemala (Mariano Galvez University of Guatemala)
3a. Avenida 9-00, Zona 2
Interior Fca. El Zapote
Guatemala City
Tels.: 534358, 534329,534252,
534296, 534339, 534348, 534271

Established in 1966, the *Universidad Mariano Galvez* was authorized to operate by both the USAC and the Council on Private Higher Education.

- **Academic calendar:** 2 semesters, February to June and July to November. Some programs may operate on a quarter or bimester system (1 bimester = 2 months).

- **Grading system:** The grading scale is 0 to 100, with 61 the minimum passing grade.

Program offered	Credential	Duration
Architecture	*licenciado*	5 years
Business Administration	*licenciado*	6.5 years

Program offered	Credential	Duration
Medical Assistant	*técnico*	2.5 years
Management	*técnico universitario*	3 years
Clinical Psychology	*licenciado*	5 years
Programming	*técnico superior*	2 years
Systems Analyst	*técnico superior*	3 years
Information Systems	*licenciado*	5 years
Marketing	*licenciado*	5 years
Nursing	*licenciado*	3 years
Theology	*licenciado*	6.5 years
Dental Surgeon	*licenciado*	5 years
Public Accounting and Auditing	*licenciado*	5 years
International Trade	*licenciado*	5.5 years
Lawyer and Notary	*licenciado*	6 years
Notary Law	*maestría*	2 years

Universidad Rafael Landívar/URL (Rafael Landívar University)
Campus Central
Vista Hermosa III, Zona 16
Guatemala City
Tels.: 380159/69, 692151, 692751
Fax: 692756

Established in 1966, the *Universidad Rafael Landívar/URL* is a private university, founded by Jesuits in 1961 and recognized by the state in 1966. It has a central campus in Guatemala City, and seven branch campuses (Antigua, Escuintla, Jutiapa, Zacapa, Retalhuleu, La Verapaz, and Quetzaltenango). The institution has a total of 11,500 students, 8,000 of whom study on the main campus. To date, over 7,000 students have graduated from the *Universidad Landívar*.

The main campus in Guatemala City contains a library, computer center, specialized laboratories for specific programs, projection and audiovisual rooms, art gallery, auditorium, chapel, bookstore, sports facilities, cafeteria, and artistic/cultural programs.

- **Admission:** Each applicant must pass an admission exam, which is given in October, November, May, and June. A secondary school diploma and application, along with the results of the admission exam, must be presented for admission. Admission to graduate programs requires a *licenciado* degree.

- **Grading:** The grade range is from 0 to 100, with a minimum grade of 61 required to pass. Each class is assigned a number of credits, based upon the number of 45-minute class meetings per week.

- **Organization:** The university is divided into eight colleges (*facultades*). The student population in the main campus is distributed among them as follows: Architecture (13%), Agricultural and Environmental Sciences (6%), Economic Sciences (39%), Legal and Social Sciences (7%), Social and Political Sciences (3%), Humanities (16%), Engineering (15%), and Theology (1%).

- **Credentials Awarded:**
  URL grants three undergraduate degrees, the *técnico universitario* (3 years), *licenciado* (5 years), *profesorado* (2.5-3 years); and two graduate degrees, *doctorado* (2 years) and *maestría* (2 years). *Ingeniero agrónomo* (engineer in agronomy) and *abogado* (attorney) degrees are considered equivalent to the *licenciado*; they are first university degrees. (See Document 5.2.)

Like other Guatemalan universities, classes at the *URL* are offered in morning, afternoon, evening, and Saturday shifts. Typically, programs at the central campus are offered either in the morning, afternoon, or both, while the branch campuses hold classes primarily on Saturdays.

Program offered	Credential	Duration
Architecture		
Graphic Design	*licenciado*	5 years
Industrial Design	*técnico universitario*	3 years
Industrial Design	*licenciado*	5 years
Architecture	*licenciado*	5 years
Agricultural and Environmental Sciences		
Cooperative Business Administration	*técnico universitario*	3.5 years
Plant Technician /Specialist in Crops	*técnico universitario*	3 years
Vegetable and Fruit Production	*técnico universitario*	3 years
Agricultural Sciences	*licenciado*	5 years
Economics		
International Trade	*técnico universitario*	3 years
Business Administration	*técnico universitario*	3 years
Publicity	*técnico universitario*	3 years
Business Administration	*licenciado*	5 years
Public Accounting and Auditing	*licenciado*	5 years
Economics	*licenciado*	5 years
Marketing	*licenciado*	5 years
Legal and Notary Sciences		
Official Interpreter	*técnico universitario*	3 years
Legal and Notary Sciences	*licenciado* (Attorney and Notary)	5 years
Political and Social Sciences		
Philosophy	*profesorado*	2.5 years
Mathematics and Physics	*profesorado*	3 years
Natural Sciences	*profesorado*	3 years
Bilingual Education	*profesorado*	3 years
Tourism Businesses	*técnico universitario*	3.5 years
Communication Sciences	*técnico universitario*	3 years
Student Counseling, Learn. Problems	*técnico universitario*	3 years
Problems of Hearing and Language	*técnico universitario*	3 years
Personnel Administration	*técnico universitario*	3 years
Communication Sciences	*licenciado*	3 years*
Letters and Philosophy	*licenciado*	5 years
Pedagogy with orientation in Administration and Educational Evaluation	*licenciado*	3years*
Psychology	*licenciado*	3years*
Educational Psychology	*licenciado*	3years*
Human Resources	*licenciado*	3years*
Pedagogy	*licenciado*	5 years
Philosophy	*doctorado*	2 years**
Preventative and Community Psychology	*maestría*	2 years**

Program offered	Credential	Duration
Engineering		
Industrial Production	*técnico universitario*	3 years
Administrative Civil Engineering	*licenciado*	6 years
Industrial Engineering	*licenciado*	5 years
Industrial Mechanical Engineering	*licenciado*	6 years
Industrial Chemical Engineering	*licenciado*	6 years
Systems and Computer Engineering	*licenciado*	5 years
Industrial Administration	*maestría-*	2.5 years
Theology		
Theology	*profesorado*	3 years
Theology	*licenciado*	2* years
Religious Sciences	*profesorado*	3 years

* After the *técnico* degree is completed.
** After the *licenciado* degree is completed.

Sample Plan of Study for *profesorado* in Mathematics and Physics - *URL*

First Semester:
Language I
Introduction to Psychology I
Logic and Study Methods
Pedagogy I
Group Psychodynamics
Mathematics I

Second Semester:
Language II
Introduction to Psychology II
Sociological Study of Guatemala
Evolutionary Psychology I
Physics I

Third Semester:
Philosophic Study of
   Man
Statistics I
Psychology of Learning
Evolutionary Psychology II
Didactic Communication
Accounting I

Fourth Semester:
Research Methodology-
Theory of Knowledge
Pedagogy II
Didactic Programming

Mathematics II

Fifth Semester
Ethics
Student Evaluation
History of Culture I
Mathematics III
Physics II

Sixth Semester:
Social Thought of the
   Church
Philosophy of Education
History of Culture II
Statistics
Seminar
Teaching Practicum

Glossary

Abogado(a). Lawyer

Arquitecto(a). Architect

Baccalaureatus in Artibus. First university degree in the Colegio Universitario, Universidad del Valle

Baccalaaureatus in Scientiis. First university degree in the Colegio Universitario, Universidad del Valle

Bachillerato or *bachiller.* First university degree in some countries; generally translated as secondary school diploma.

Carrera. Program of study/major/specialization

Carrera corta. Short program of study

Carrera intermedia. Intermediate program of study

Cirujano Dentista. Dental Surgeon

Colegio Profesional. Professional Association

Doctor/Doctorado. Doctor, usually of medicine or dentistry (a first university degree in Central America); also may be a graduate level doctorate in philosophy.

Economista. Economist

Equivalencia/Equi. Equivalence

Especialización, Especializado en... Specialization, Specialist in...

Ingeniero(a)/Ingeniería. Engineer(ing)

Licenciado(a)/Licenciatura. Licentiate, generally first university degree

Maestría. Master's

Maestro/a. Teacher

Matutina. Morning schedule

Nocturna. Evening schedule

Pensum. List of required courses and prerequisites for a specific program; also called *plan de estudios* (study plan)

Perito. Expert

Profesorado. Teaching degree

Profesor(a) en (specialization). Teacher of (specialization)

Sabatina. Saturday schedule

Técnico. Technician (note: may be a secondary-level degree)

Técnico universitario. University-level technician

Título. Title/degree

Vespertina. Afternoon schedule

	PENSUM PROFESIONAL	
No. Código	**Materias Fundadas**	**Materias Fundantes**
	Séptimo Semestre:	
056	Derecho Administrativo II........................	Derecho Administrativo I
058	Derecho Procesal Civil I..........................	Derecho Procesal Penal I
060	Derecho Mercantil I..............................	Derecho Civil IV
062	Derecho del Trabajo I............................	Derecho Civil IV y Teoría del Proceso
084	Derecho Notarial I...............................	Derecho Civil IV
	Octavo Semestre:	
064	Derecho Procesal Civil II........................	Derecho Procesal Civil I
066	Derecho Mercantil II.............................	Derecho Mercantil I
068	Derecho del Trabajo II	Derecho del Trabajo I
089	Derecho Procesal Administrativo.................	Derecho Administrativo II
085	Derecho Notarial II..............................	Derecho Notarial I y Derecho Mercantil I
	Noveno Semestre:	
070	Derecho Internacional Público	Derecho Procesal Administrativo y Derecho Mercantil II.
071	Derecho Procesal del Trabajo	Derecho del Trabajo II, Derecho Procesal Civil I y Derecho Procesal Administrativo.
073	Derecho de Integración	Sociología del Desarrollo
076	Hacienda Pública.................................	Derecho Procesal Administrativo y Derecho Mercantil II.
086	Derecho Notarial III	Derecho Notarial II y Derecho Mercantil II
	Décimo Semestre:	
078	Filosofía del Derecho	Derecho Procesal Civil II, Derecho Mercantil II, Derecho del Trabajo II y Derecho Internacional Público.
087	Derecho Notarial IV	Derecho Notarial III
082	Derecho Financiero...............................	Hacienda Pública
074	Derecho Internacional Privado	Derecho Internacional Público
081	Seminario Sobre Problemas Sociales	

PRERREQUISITOS: *Para evitar nulidades en su curriculum de estudios, el alumno debe observar estrictamente el orden de prerrequisitos y en ningún caso aprobar una materia fundada antes que la materia fundante.*

Este documento recoge el Pénsum de Estudios de la Facultad de Ciencias Jurídicas y Sociales aprobado en 1971 y sus modificaciones introducidas en 1988, 1990 y 1992.

Guatemala, enero de 1993.

Document 5.1 Study plan for undergraduate Law concentration at the *San Carlos University of Guatemala/USAC*. Prerequisites are also indicated. There are few electives in the program.

258-90 GOMEZ MATIAS			ALBERTO JAVIER	1
FACULTAD HUMANIDADES		UNIVERSIDAD RAFAEL LANDIVAR		
		DEPARTAMENTO PEDAGOGIA Y PSICOLOGIA		

		Nombre del Curso y Créditos	Inscripción	Aprobado	Nota
1	Q2101	Pedagogía General	23.1.90	26.5.90	73
2	Q2102	Elementos de Lógica y Conocimiento	"	9.6.90	74
3	Q2103	Psicología General	"	2.6.90	93
4	Q2104	Lenguaje I	"	2.6.90	77
5	Q2120	Estudio Sociológico de Guatemala.	"	9.6.90	86
6	P40	Lenguaje	"	9.6.90	63
7	Q2105	Estudio Filos. de Hombre.	2.7.90	3.11.90	85
8	Q2106	Psicol. del Niño y del Adolescente.	"	10.3.91	79
9	Q2107	Didáctica General	"	4.11.90	84
10	Q2121	Sistemas Ped. I	"	3.11.90	74
11	Q2117	Lenguaje II	"	17.11.90	72
12	P30	Tec. de Investigación Social.	"	4.11.90	69
13	P17	Q'anjobal I	"	18.11.90	85
14	Q2108	Estudio Filosófico del Mundo y la Ciencia	26.1.91	25.5.91	83
15	Q2123	Sist. Pedagógicos II	"	21.7.91	69
16	Q2124	Programación por Objetivos	"	1.6.91	69
17	Q2126	Didáctica Especial	"	1.6.91	68
18	Q2128	Administración y Legislación Escolar.	"	8.6.91	62
19	P18	Q'anjobal II	"	8.6.91	75
20	P39	Antropología Social	"	8.6.91	63
21	Q2110	Metodología de la Investigación	22.6.91	9.11.91	72
22	Q2111	Planeamiento Didáctico	"	26.X.91	79
23	Q2122	Psicología de la Personalidad	"	2.11.91	80
24	Q2133	Material Didáctico	"	2.11.91	82
25	Q2114	Técnicas de Evaluación Escolar	"	9.11.91	71
26	P19	Qanjobal III	"	25.X.91	72
27	P32	Sociología del Desarrollo	"	17.1.92	78
28	Q2112	Etica	18.1.92	6.6.92	71
29	Q2113	Estadística I	"	23.5.92	79
30	Q2109	Psicología del Aprendizaje	"	30.5.92	72
31	Q2127	Psicología Social	"	30.5.92	80
32	Q2131	Elaboración de Pruebas Educativas	"	23.5.92	88
33	Q2116	Práctica Docente	"	21.11.92	A
34	P20	Q'anjob'al IV	"	29.5.92	95
35	P34	Economía Guatemalteca	"	29.5.92	76

No. Reg. Primer Apellido Segundo Apellido   Nombres

UNIVERSIDAD RAFAEL LANDIVAR
Quetzaltenango

PROFESORADO EN PEDAGOGIA Y PSICOLOGIA.

ALBERTO JAVIER GOMEZ MATIAS.

Departamento de PROFESORADO EN PEDAGOGIA Y PSICOLOGIA. EN ESTA CERTIFICACION NO VALEN TACHONES

ULTIMA LINEA

DIRECTOR DE REGISTRO

Lic. José Luís Domínguez Guzmán

APROBACION DE CURSOS:

minimo de 51 pts. hasta Octubre/86
minimo de 60 pts. hasta Mayo/86
minimo de 61 pts. desde Octubre/86

El presente documento es una copia fiel de las calificaciones obtenidas por el estudiante ALBERTO JAVIER GOMEZ MATIAS. Departamento de HUMANIDADES Número de Carnet 258 - 90 , en la Facultad de HUMANIDADES

Todas las clases son del ciclo semestral, calificados sobre cien (100) puntos para aprobar el curso, con un mínimo, según se indica,

BORRONES, NI ENMIENDAS:

LA FIRMA Y SELLO DEBEN SER ORIGINALES EN EL ANVERSO Y REVERSO EN EL CASO DE QUE ESTE SE UTILICE

Quetzaltenango. 7 de Enero de 1,993.-

Document 5.2 The student is enrolled in a program for indigenous Guatemalans, at the _Universidad Rafael Landivar/URL_, which includes courses in Q`anjobal, his native language.

Chapter 6
The Educational System of Honduras

The Country

Honduras is a the second largest Central American nation (after Nicaragua), bordered on the west by Guatemala, the south by El Salvador and Nicaragua, and on the north by the Caribbean Sea. The national capital, Tegucigalpa, is located in the south central section of the country, set in rugged, mountainous territory. The most important city economically and industrially in Honduras is San Pedro Sula, on the northern coast. San Pedro Sula has traditionally been the principal site for agricultural cultivation, and has also become the home of numerous industrial plants in a now burgeoning free trade zone.

The People

Although Spanish is the official language of Honduras, speakers of English, Creole, and Garifuna can be found on the coast and also in the nearby Bay Islands. With a per capita income estimated at approximately $516 (1991, U.S. State Department), Hondurans are among the poorest of the region's inhabitants. However, despite the lack of economic prosperity, the country has produced a number of noteworthy artists and writers. Honduras has a particularly active cultural life, with numerous galleries, several artists' communities, and many special events sponsored by the *Universidad Nacional Autónoma de Honduras.*

Postsecondary Education

On September 17, 1989, the Honduras National Congress approved a new Law of Higher Education, which took effect a month later. The law reiterated previously existing statutes about the authority of the *Universidad Nacional Autónoma de Honduras/UNAH* (National Autonomous University of Honduras), which has the exclusive responsibility of organizing, directing, and developing professional and higher education. All programs and institutions in postsecondary education must be approved by the *UNAH*, a task it carries out through the *Consejo de Educación Superior* (Council of Higher Education). The 1989 law also standardized academic calendars, institutional processes for recognition, and minimum requirements for programs of study.

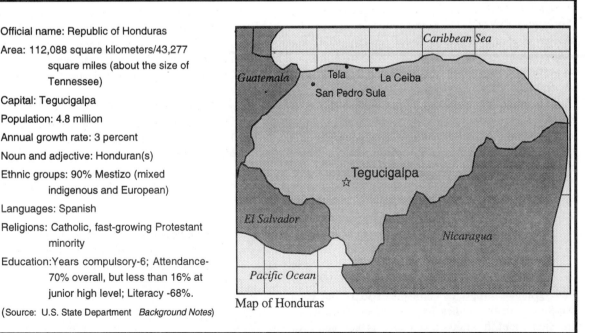

Official name: Republic of Honduras

Area: 112,088 square kilometers/43,277 square miles (about the size of Tennessee)

Capital: Tegucigalpa

Population: 4.8 million

Annual growth rate: 3 percent

Noun and adjective: Honduran(s)

Ethnic groups: 90% Mestizo (mixed indigenous and European)

Languages: Spanish

Religions: Catholic, fast-growing Protestant minority

Education: Years compulsory-6; Attendance- 70% overall, but less than 16% at junior high level; Literacy -68%.

(Source: U.S. State Department *Background Notes*)

Map of Honduras

Following is a paraphrased synopsis of the salient points covered by the 1989 educational law (Decree Number 142-89): The *Universidad Nacional Autónoma de Honduras* remains an autonomous and decentralized State institution which has the exclusive responsibility of organizing, directing, and developing professional and higher education. The *UNAH* carries out this responsibility through the *Consejo de Educación Superior* (Council of Higher Education).

The *Consejo de Educación Superior* consists of: *UNAH's* rector; six representatives of the *UNAH*; six elected rectors or directors of centers of higher education, at least three of whom must represent private institutions; and the head of the Higher Education Board. Each member serves a 2-year term. They are elected by a larger body of rectors, directors, and representatives of all recognized institutions of higher education, the *Consejo Técnico Consultivo*.

The *Consejo de Educación Superior* creates higher education policies and enforces the law of higher education. It also approves the creation and functioning of all higher education centers, public and private, and the opening, functioning, merging, or suspension of programs of study, schools, colleges (*facultades*), institutes, research centers, curricula, and special programs.

The *UNAH* is responsible, by agreement, for the granting of academic degrees from all Honduran institutions, public and private. Validation of studies from other countries, recognition of study programs, and academic equivalencies are also carried out by the *UNAH* in accordance with established norms. The *UNAH* maintains a registry of degrees and diplomas of programs of higher education; only people with valid degrees can engage in certain professional activities.

The 1989 law recognizes the *Escuela Nacional de Agricultura/ENA* and the *Escuela Nacional de Ciencias Forestales/ESNACIFOR* as institutions of higher education. It also recognizes, as of January 1990, the *Universidad Pedagógica Nacional "Francisco Morazán"* as officially replacing the *Escuela Superior del Profesorado "Francisco Morazán."*

There are four types of institutions of higher education in Honduras: universities, institutes, schools, and academies. Institutes are distinguished by the characteristic of offering one academic area, but they may add other areas leading to the training of professionals. Schools (*Escuelas*) are responsible for one academic area, with the emphasis also in training. Academies (*Academias*) are vocational programs.

Credits

The law establishes that a unit of academic measure (*unidad de medida académica* or *UMA*) for undergraduate programs corresponds to 1 hour each week of academic studies, for a period of 15 weeks, or its equivalent if another calendar is adopted. An academic hour is equal to 50 classroom minutes. When applied to laboratories, workshops, seminars, or field work, the credit must represent 3 hours of academic work in the same period. The credit, therefore, is meant to represent 1 hour in the classroom plus 2 hours of preparation and homework.

Fulltime status for undergraduates consists of at least 16 credits per term, or 48 hours per week. For graduate students, full time status is defined as 12 credits per term. For graduate programs, 1 credit is equivalent to 1 hour in the classroom plus 3 hours of preparation or homework, or 4 hours of directed academic work.

Calendar

Academic years may be organized in any of the following configurations: one period, with a minimum of 32 weeks of classes; periods of a minimum of 18 weeks in each; periods of a minimum of 15 weeks in each; periods with a minimum of 11 weeks in each; or periods with a minimum of 9 weeks of classes in each.

Degrees

University degrees, and the corresponding credits required, are established as follows:

1) *Carrera Corta*: 80 to 100 credits, 2-year
   program.
2) *Licenciado*: 160 or more credits.
3) *Doctorado en Medicina y Cirugía*

A minimum of 320 credits, with a duration of 6 to 8 years, is required for training in medicine, teaching, and scientific research.

Note that the *bachiller universitario*, one of the traditional first university degrees in Honduras, has been eliminated under the new law. It is being phased out gradually and current documents continue to contain the credential in some institutions.

Graduate-level (*postgrado*) degrees offered are:

1) *Especialidad*: 30 to 90 credits beyond the *licenciado*, with a duration of 1-3 years. *Especialidad Médica*: 90 credits beyond the *doctorado en medicina*, with an additional 3 years minimum.

2) *Maestría*: 40 to 52 credits beyond the *licenciado*, for 1.5 to 2 years.

3) *Doctorado*: From 52 to 70 credits beyond the *licenciado*, or from 25 to 30 credits beyond a graduate degree, with a minimum of 2 additional years.

Institutional Profiles

Escuela Nacional de Agricultura/ENA
(National Agricultural School)
Apartado Postal No 9
Catacamas, Olancho
Tel: 95-4133, 4134, 4135
Fax: 95-4134

Established in January 20, 1950, and began offering classes in 1952. Authorization to operate: *Consejo de Educación Superior*

- **Grading system**: 0 to 100%; minimum passing grade: 60%; average required for graduation: 70%.
- **Enrollment** (1994): 205, all study full time (5-6 courses or 18-22 credits per academic cycle). An average of 45 students graduate each year.

- **Faculty** (1994): 36 fulltime professors; 7 with *maestría* degrees, 26 with *licenciado* degrees, and 3 with *técnico* degrees.

- **Credentials awarded:** *agrónomo* (3-year degree); *ingeniero agrónomo* (4-year degree as of 1994.) The *Escuela Nacional de Agricultura/ENA* is a public institution established in 1952 under the name *Escuela Granja Demostrativa* (Model Farm School). The 1989 Law of Education stipulates that the school's programs are considered university-level courses. Since 1978, the school has offered an intermediate technical degree and a 4-year *ingeniero agrónomo* degree.

Escuela Nacional de Ciencias Forestales/ ESNACIFOR (National School of Forestry Sciences)
Apartado No. 2
Departamento de Comayagua
Siguatepeque

Established on January 6, 1969, the *ESNACIFOR* is a public, university-level institution founded by the Honduran government with assistance from the United Nations. Students graduate with the title of *dasónomo*, a 3-year technical forestry degree. Programs of study are offered in Forestry Management, Wood Utilization, Forestry Promotion and Extension, Forestry Administration, and Environmental Issues.

Universidad Católica de Honduras "Nuestra Señora Reina de la Paz" ("Our Lady Queen of Peace" Catholic University of Honduras)
Apartado Postal 4473

Calle El Seminario No. 1501
Barrio Casamata
Tegucigalpa
Tel.: 38-6794 to 96
Fax: 38-6797

Established and authorized by the *Consejo de Educación Superior* to grant degrees: December 4, 1992

- **Academic calendar:** 3 periods per year, beginning in January (See Document 6.1)

- **Grading Scale:** 0 to 100; Minimum passing grade: 70; Cumulative average required for graduation: 75.

- **Enrollment:** 225

- **Faculty:** 22 (14 fulltime) 5 with doctorate degrees, 13 with master's degrees, and 4 with bachelor's degree or equivalent.

- **Admissions:** secondary school degree, admissions examination.

- **Credentials awarded:** *licenciado, ingeniero,* and *postgrado* (postgraduate studies). *licenciado* and *ingeniero* degrees require at least 4 years of study.

Programs offered	Credential	Duration
Banking and Finance	*licenciado*	12 periods (4 years)
Computer Sciences	*licenciado*	12 periods (4 years)
Environmental Sciences	*licenciado*	12 periods (4 years)
International Relations and Diplomacy	*licenciado*	12 periods (4 years)
Total Quality Management	*post-grado*	6 modules (duration unreported)

Universidad de San Pedro Sula/USPS
(San Pedro Sula University)
Colonia Colombia
Apdo Postal 1064
San Pedro Sula
Tels.: 52-2277, 52-3213, 52-3279
Fax: 53-1889

The *Universidad de San Pedro Sula,* located in Honduras' second-largest city, was founded and authorized by the *Consejo de Educación Superior* to grant degrees on August 21, 1978. In addition to classroom and laboratory facilities, the university has 33 personal computers for student use and a working farm for field experience.

- **Enrollment:** 1,536

- **Faculty:** 140 (134 part-time)

- **Academic calendar:** 2 semesters, January to December

- **Grading system:** 0 to 100. Minimum grade of 66% to pass a course, 76% cumulative average to graduate.

- **Credentials awarded:** The institution offers *licenciado* degrees in the following areas:

Programs offered	Duration
Administrative Computer Science	4 years
Agronomy	4.5 years
Architecture	4.5 years
Business Administration	4 years
Communications	4 years
Industrial Engineering	4.5 years
Law	4.5 years

Universidad José Cecilio del Valle/UJCV
(José Cecilio del Valle University)
6a Avenida
No. 603
Barrio Buenos Aires
Apartado 917
Tegucigalpa
Tel.: 22-8961, 22-8963, 37-7807
Fax: 37-0575

Founded and authorized by the *Consejo de Educación Superior* to operate: February 1978 (*UJCV* degrees are recognized by the *Universidad Nacional de Honduras.*

- **Calendar:** 4 trimesters of 11 weeks each, beginning in January

- **Enrollment:** 411 (385 graduates as of 1994)

- **Faculty:** 43 (35 part-time)

- **Admissions requirements:** Applicants to the university must show proof of secondary school graduation and submit secondary school transcripts. First-year students are required to take 2 trimesters of non-credit math and Spanish. A grade of 65 must be earned to progress into an academic program.

- **Grading scale:** 0 to 100, with corresponding letter grades and quality points:

A	95-100	(4.0)	Excellent (*Excelente*)
B+	90-94	(3.5)	Very Good (*Muy Bueno*)
B	85-89	(3.0)	Good (*Bueno*)
C+	80-84	(2.5)	Average (*Regular*)
C	75-79	(2.0)	Minimum for graduation (*Mínimo de graduación*)
D+	60-74	(1.5)	Minimum for good standing (*Mínimo de permanencia*)
D	65-69	(1.0)	Minimum to pass a class (*Mínimo de paso*)
F	0-64	(0)	Failing (*Aplazado*)

- **Organization:** Faculties of Arts and Sciences, Administration, Engineering, Data Processing, Language. Fulltime students take at least 12 credits per semester, and 1 credit hour is equivalent to a 90-minute class. Transcripts show failing grades, and the overall average includes failures. A credit (*crédito*, also known as a *unidad valorativa* or *u.v.*) is equivalent to 1 hour of class per week for 11 weeks.

- **Credentials Awarded:**

Técnico (2 years, 80 to 100 credits):

Licenciado (4 years, 160 to 180 credits), construction, agricultural administration, electronic data processing, forestry administration, graphic design, industrial management, interior design, journalism, tourism, tourism administration.

- *Ingeniero* (4 years, 160 to 180 credits): agricultural civil engineering, construction engineering, computer systems, forestry, industrial engineering.

***Universidad Nacional Autónoma de Honduras/UNAH* (National Autonomous University of Honduras)**
Main Campus:
Ciudad Universitaria
Tegucigalpa
Tel.: 32-2208

San Pedro Sula Branch:
***Centro Universitario Regional del Norte* (CURN)**
Carretera a Puerto Cortes
San Pedro Sula, Cortes
Tel: 57-61-56, 53-21-48, 53-14-63
Fax: 57-61-57

***Sistema Universitario de Educación a Distancia/SUED* (University System of Distance Education)**

- Established: 1847. Authorization to operate: *Consejo de Educación Superior*

  Calendar: February to December

- **Grading system**: 0 to 100%, as follows;

90-100	Outstanding	(*Sobresaliente*)
80-89	Very Good	(*Muy Bueno*)
60-79	Good	(*Bueno*)
0-59	Failing	(*Reprobado*)

  Minimum passing grade: 60%; average required for graduation: 60%.

- **Enrollment:** 9,767.

- **Faculty:** 418 professors; 218 full time, 19 part time, 177 hired hourly

- **Academic calendar:** The university functions on a trimester system, from February to November.

- **Credentials awarded**: *licenciado* (4-year degree), *maestría* (2-4 years). Over 20,000 degrees have been awarded since the university was founded. The four branches of *UNAH* are abbreviated as follows: Main campus in Tegucigalpa: *UNAH;* San Pedro Sula campus: *CURN*; La Ceiba campus: *CURLA*; Distance education division: *SUED*.

Program of Study	Duration (years)	Location(s)
Administrative Computer Sci.	4.5	UNAH
Agricultural Administration	4.5	SUED
Agricultural Economics	5	CURLA
Agronomy	5	CURLA
Architecture	5.5	UNAH
Art	4	UNAH
Banking Administration	5	UNAH
Biology	5.5	UNAH
Business Administration	5	UNAH, CURN
Chemical Engineering	5	UNAH
Chemistry	4	CURN
Chemistry and Pharmacy	5	UNAH
Civil Engineering	6†	UNAH, CURN
Construction Engineering	2	UNAH
Customs Administration	4.5	UNAH
Dentistry	6‡	UNAH
Economics	5	UNAH, CURN
Economics	2**	UNAH
Electrical Engineering	5	CURN, UNAH
Foreign Languages with concentration in English, French	4	UNAH
Forestry Engineering	5	CURLA
History	5	UNAH
Industrial Engineering	4.5	UNAH, CURN
Journalism	4	UNAH, CURN
Law	5	UNAH, CURN
Letters	5	UNAH
Mathematics	4	UNAH, CURN
Medicine	7	UNAH
Mercantile Law	2††	UNAH
Mechanical Engineering	5	UNAH, CURN
Microbiology	5	UNAH
Music	5	UNAH
Nursing	5.5	UNAH, CURN, CURLA, SUED
Pedagogy	5	UNAH, CURN
Pedagogy	4	SUED
Philosophy	4	UNAH
Physical Education	5	UNAH
Physics	4	UNAH
Psychology	4.5	UNAH
Public Accounting	5	UNAH, CURN
Public Accounting	1.5‡‡	UNAH
Public Administration	5	UNAH, CURN
Social Sciences	4***	CURN
Social Work	5	UNAH
Social Work	2†††	UNAH
Specialties in Medicine		UNAH

* In the process of being phased out under the new education law.
† Includes thesis
‡ Includes social service)
** *postgrado*
†† *doctorado*, after *liciendo*
‡‡ *maestría*
*** *bachillier universitario*
††† *postgrado*

Universidad Pedagógica Nacional "Francisco Morazán"/UPN ("Francisco Morazán" National Pedagogic University)
Apdo. Postal 3394
Tegucigalpa
Tel.: 32-8037, 31-1257, 32-7417

The *UPN*, formerly known as the *Escuela Superior del Profesorado "Francisco Morazán"*, was established in 1956 as a public institution. It has traditionally served as the foremost teacher training school in Honduras.

Since 1990, when the institution officially became a university, its programs of study have been in a period of transition. While the school traditionally offered two degrees (*bachiller universitario* and *profesorado*), it now will award only the 5-year *licenciado*. There are now several programs in place, including competency examinations, to help *bachiller universitario* and *profesorado* students qualify for the *licenciado* program.

In addition to the main campus in Tegucigalpa and branch in San Pedro Sula, *UPN* has eight extension centers: Choluteca, La Ceiba, Tela, Santa Rosa de Copán, La Esperanza, Danli, Juticalpa, and La Paz. It also has a distance education program.

Programs offered	Credential	Duration
Commercial Education	*licenciado*	5 years
Educational Administration	*licenciado*	5 years
Educational Counseling	*licenciado*	5 years
English Letters and Lang.	*licenciado*	5 years
Industrial Education	*licenciado*	5 years
Mathematics	*licenciado*	5 years
Natural Sciences	*licenciado*	5 years
Physical Education	*licenciado*	5 years
Preschool Education	*licenciado*	5 years
Spanish Letters and Lang.	*licenciado*	5 years
Special Education	*licenciado*	5 years
Technical Education	*licenciado*	5 years
Technical Education for the Home	*licenciado*	5 years

Universidad Tecnológica Centroamericana/ UNITEC (Central American Technological University)
Frente a Residencial Honduras
Tegucigalpa
Fax: 31-3258

Authorized by *Consejo de Educación Superior* to grant degrees: December 17, 1986

* **Facilities:** Classroom buildings, computer center, with Novell netware network; IBM AS/400 with 10 terminals. Information Center, which consists of technical support services, library, audiovisual department, counseling services, and Chemistry and Physics laboratories.

Programs offered:	Credential:
Industrial Administration	*licenciado*
Business Administration	*licenciado*
Management Computer Systems	*licenciado*
Marketing	*licenciado*
Computer Systems	*ingeniero*
Industrial Engineering	*ingeniero*
Systems Engineering	*ingeniero*
Business Computer Systems	*técnico superior universitario*
Marketing, Sales	*técnico superior universitario*
Communications, Advertising	*técnico superior universitario*

Graduate level programs:
Maestría in Business Administration with a concentration in Marketing
Maestría in Business Administration with a concentration in Finance
Maestría in Business Administration with a concentration in Human Resources
Maestría in International Marketing

* **Admissions requirements:** 1. High school degree; 2. Completed application; 3. Photographs and identification card or birth certificate.

Other institutions:

Escuela Agrícola Panamericana/"Zamorano" (Pan American Agricultural School)
Apartado Postal 93
Tegucigalpa
Tel.: 76-6140 and 76-6150
Fax: 32-8543 and 76-6240
E-mail: eapbwp@huracan.cr

Established in 1942, the *Escuela Agrícola Panamericana*, or *Zamorano* (as it is commonly known), is an autonomous institution that was incorporated in the state of Delaware. It is not Honduran by definition, and it serves a variety of students from throughout Latin America. The school, founded by the United Fruit Company, is a private, non-profit, international agricultural school serving the need for agricultural experts in the Americas. In 1994, the student body had representatives from 16 countries, 20 percent of whom were Hondurans.

* **Academic calendar:** Three 15-week academic periods, as follows: January to April, May to August, September to November

* **Enrollment:** 675 (fulltime); approximately 22 percent female.

* **Faculty:** 97 (fulltime), 29 with doctorates, 27 with master's degrees, 33 with first university degree (*bachilliers* or *licenciado*).

* **Credentials Awarded:** Since 1986, *Zamorano* has offered a 4- to 5-year agronomy degree (*ingeniero agrónomo*), in addition to its 33-month agronomist (*agrónomo)* degree. The *ingeniero agrónomo* degree was officially recognized in 1994 by the Honduran Council of Higher Education. The latter program requires a thesis, while the *agrónomo* degree does not. (See Document 6.2)

  The program followed by *Zamorano* students combines 25 weekly hours of classroom and laboratory work with 24 weekly hours of field training. Students spend 4 hours each day in the field, from Monday through Saturday. (See Document 6.3)

Grading System:

%	Grade	Points	Description
90-100	A	4.00	Excellent (*Excelente*)
86-89	B+	3.50	Very Good (*Muy Bueno*)
80-85	B	3.00	Good (*Bueno*)
76-79	C+	2.50	Average (*Regular*)
70-75	C	2.00	Average (*Regular*)
66-69	D+	1.50	Passing (*Suficiente*)
0-59	F	0.00	Failing (*Insuficiente*)

Grades followed by an "R" have been obtained after a "rehabilitation" examination that is offered when students fail a course. One period credit (shown on transcript) is equivalent to 1 hour of class, 2 hours of lab work, or 4 hours of field work per week. A minimum 2.0 cumulative grade point average is required for graduation.

- **Admissions:** Applicants for the *agrónomo* program must possess one of the following secondary or postsecondary degrees: *perito mercantíl, maestro(a) de educación primaria* or *bachiller*; or enrollment in final year of secondary studies. Students must be single and less than 23 years old at the time of enrollment. All candidates must pass an admissions examination and an interview. Applicants for the fourth year *ingeniero agrónomo* program must hold a minimum cumulative grade point average of 2.3 in the *agrónomo* program.

Glossary

Abogado(a). Lawyer

Arquitecto(a). Architect

Bachillerato or *bachiller*. First university degree in some countries; generally translated as secondary school diploma.

Bachiller universitario. University-level *bachiller*, currently being phased out in Honduras

Carrera. Program of study/major/specialization

Cirujano Dentista. Dental Surgeon

Cirugía. Surgery

Consejo de Educación Superior. Council of Higher Education

Doctor/Doctorado. Doctor, usually of medicine or dentistry (a first university degree in Central America); also may be a graduate level doctorate in philosophy, a credential that is emerging in Central American higher education

Especialización. Specialization

Ingeniero(a)/Ingeniería. Engineer(ing)

Licenciado(a)/Licenciatura. Licentiate, generally first university degree

Maestría. Master's

Maestro/a. Teacher

Pensum. List of required courses and prerequisites for a specific program; also called *plan de estudios* (study plan)

Perito. Expert

Profesorado. Teaching degree

Profesor(a) en (specialization). Teacher of (specialization)

Técnico. Technician

Título. Title/ degree

Unidad de medida académica/ UMA. Unit of academic measure, equal to 1 hour per week of classroom time

UNIVERSIDAD CATOLICA DE HONDURAS
"NUESTRA SEÑORA REINA DE LA PAZ"

CERTIFICACION DE ESTUDIOS

El Infrascrito Secretario General de la Universidad Católica de Honduras "Nuestra Señora Reina de la Paz", por este medio **CERTIFICA:** que ___ con registro No. ___, está matriculada en esta Universidad en la Carrera de **LICENCIATURA EN RELACIONES INTERNACIONALES Y DIPLOMACIA** habiendo cursado las siguientes asignaturas:

Código	Asignatura	Créd.	Periodo	Año	Nota	Obs.
ES-101	Español	3	Primero	93	83	Apr.
MT-101	Matemática	4	Primero	93	84	Apr.
SC-101	Sociología	3	Primero	93	79	Apr.
IF-101	Informática	3	Primero	93	86	Apr.
FI-101	Filosofía	3	Primero	93	88	Apr.
ES-201	Exp. Oral E.	3	Segundo	93	93	Apr.
MT-201	Pre-Cálculo	4	Segundo	93	80	Apr.
IF-201	Informática II	3	Segundo	93	86	Apr.
PS-101	Psicología	3	Segundo	93	89	Apr.
CR-201	Hom. Fte. Vida	3	Segundo	93	80	Apr.
HS-101	Hist. Hond.	3	Tercero	93	93	Apr.
MT-302	Estadística I	4	Tercero	93	85	Apr.
RI-301	Sist. Int. I.	4	Tercero	93	83	Apr.
RI-302	Sist. Pol. H.	3	Tercero	93	86	Apr.
FR-101	Francés I.	3	Tercero	93	94	Apr.
FI-102	Ciencia y T.	3	Primero	94	87	Apr.
FR-201	Francés II.	3	Primero	94	90	Apr.
MT-301	Lógica MT.	3	Primero	94	85	Apr.
RI-401	Sist.Int. II	4	Primero	94	94	Apr.
RI-403	Pol. Ext. H.	3	Primero	94	95	Apr.

TOTAL CREDITOS:::::::::::::::::::::::::::::::::::::65::::::::::::
INDICE ACADEMICO::::::::::::::::::::::::::::::::::87:::::::::::

Y para los fines que convenga al interesado, se extiende la presente en la Ciudad de Tegucigalpa, M.D.C., a los veinticinco días del mes de mayo de mil novecientos noventa y cuatro.

LIC. EDGAR HANDAL FACUSSE
Secretario General.

Calle Seminario No. 1501
Colonia, Tegucigalpa, M.D.C.
Honduras, Centroamérica

Teléfonos : (504) 38-6794 al 96
Fax (504) 38-6797

Apartado Postal 4
Tegucigalpa, M.C
Honduras, Centroar

Document 6.1 Partial transcript for the trimesterly *Universidad Católica de Honduras "Nuestra Señora Reina de la Paz"* **("Our Lady Queen of Peace" Catholic University of Honduras).**

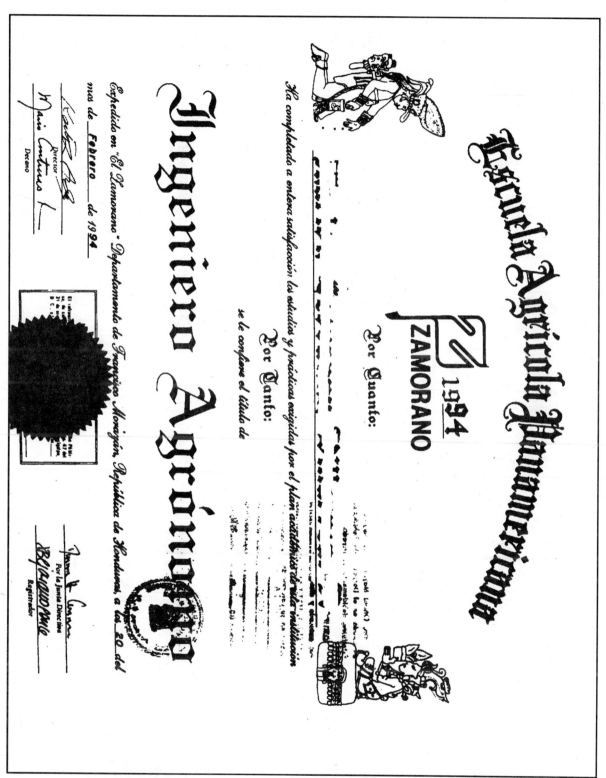

Document 6.2 Unlike the agrònomo credential, this *Escuela Agrícola Panamericana/ "Zamorano"* (Pan American Agricultural School) ingeniero agrónomo program requires that students complete a thesis for graduation.

NAME: [illegible] **CLASS: 1991**

ESCUELA AGRICOLA PANAMERICANA
REGISTRO DE NOTAS OBTENIDAS EN CLASES
REGISTER OF GRADES OBTAINED IN CLASSES

I SEMESTER

COURSE / CLASE	CREDIT HOURS	GRADE NOTA
Biología / Biology	4	C+
Botánica / Botany	3	C+
Comunicación I / Communication I	3	C
Deporte I / Sports I	1	A
Inglés I / English I	2	A
Introd. a la prod. y prot. vegetal / Introd. to plant prod. and prot.	1	C
Matemática I / Mathematics I	4	A
Laboratorio de Horticultura I / Horticulture Field Laboratory I	5	B+
TOTAL	**23**	

II SEMESTER

COURSE / CLASE	CREDIT HOURS	GRADE NOTA
Deporte II / Sports II	1	B+
Inglés II / English II	2	B
Matemática II / Mathematics II	4	A
Química Inorgánica / Inorganic Chemistry	4	C
Taxonomía de Plantas / Plant Taxonomy	3	C+
Zoología / Zoology	3	B
Laboratorio de Horticultura II / Horticulture Field Laboratory II	5	B+
TOTAL	**22**	

III SEMESTER

COURSE / CLASE	CREDIT HOURS	GRADE NOTA
Inglés III / English III	2	B
Introducción a Suelos / Introduction to Soils	4	C+
Matemática III / Mathematics III	4	A
Olericultura I / Vegetable Production I	3	D+
Propagación de Plantas / Plant Propagation	3	D
Química Orgánica / Organic Chemistry	3	C
Laboratorio de Horticultura III / Horticulture Field Laboratory III	5	B+
TOTAL	**24**	

IV SEMESTER

COURSE / CLASE	CREDIT HOURS	GRADE NOTA
Agronomía I / Agronomy I	3	C+
Contabilidad Gral. y Agrícola / General & Farm Accounting	3	D
Fertilidad de Suelos / Soil Fertility	3	B
Física / Physics	3	C+
Fisiología Vegetal / Plant Physiology	3	B
Inglés IV / English IV	2	C
Maquinaria Agrícola / Farm Machinery	3	C
Laboratorio de Agronomía I / Agronomy Field Laboratory I	5	B
TOTAL	**25**	

V SEMESTER

COURSE / CLASE	CREDIT HOURS	GRADE NOTA
Bioquímica / Biochemistry	3	D+
Entomología / Entomology	3	C
Fruticultura I (General) / Fruit Crops I (General)	3	C
Inglés V / English V	2	D+
Introducción a la Estadística / Introduction to Statistics	3	D
Microbiología / Microbiology	3	D
Laboratorio de Agronomía II / Agronomy Field Laboratory II	5	B
TOTAL	**22**	

VI SEMESTER

COURSE / CLASE	CREDIT HOURS	GRADE NOTA
Agronomía II / Agronomy II	3	D
Anatomía y Fis. de los Anim. Dom. / Domestic Animal Anatomy & Physiology	3	D
Economía General y Agrícola / General & Agricultural Economics	3	D+
Inglés VI / English VI	2	D
Fitopatología / Plant Pathology	3	C+
Genética / Genetics	3	C
Prog. de Producción Independiente / Independent Production Program	3	C+
Laboratorio de Agronomía III / Agronomy Field Laboratory III	5	B
TOTAL	**25**	

VII SEMESTER

COURSE / CLASE	CREDIT HOURS	GRADE NOTA
Alimentos y Alimentación / Feeds and Feeding	4	C+
Conservación y Manejo de Suelos / Soil Conservation & Management	3	D
Ecología / Ecology	—	—
Introd. a la Prod. Animal I / Introd. to Animal Production I	3	C
Pastos y Forrajes / Forage & Pasture Science	3	D
Elective I / Refer to Observation Below	3	C
Elective II / Refer to Observation Below	3	B
Laboratorio de Zootecnia I / Animal Science Field Laboratory I	5	B+
TOTAL	**24**	

VIII SEMESTER

COURSE / CLASE	CREDIT HOURS	GRADE NOTA
Extensión y Desarrollo Rural I / Extension & Rural Development I	3	B
Introd. a la Prod. Animal II / Introd. to Animal Production II	3	C
Riegos y Drenajes / Irrigation & Drainage	3	B+
Sanidad Animal / Animal Health	3	D
Elective I / Refer to Observation Below	3	D+
Elective II / Refer to Observation Below	3	D+
Laboratorio de Zootecnia II / Animal Science Field Laboratory II	5	B+
TOTAL	**23**	

IX SEMESTER

COURSE / CLASE	CREDIT HOURS	GRADE NOTA
Agronomía III / Agronomy III	3	C+
Comunicación II / Communication II	3	B
Manejo Integrado de Plagas / Integrated Pest Management	3	D+
Procesamiento de Productos Pecuarios / Animal Products Processing	3	C
Elective I / Refer to Observation Below	3	B
Elective II / Refer to Observation Below	3	B
Laboratorio de Zootecnia III / Animal Science Field Laboratory III	5	A
TOTAL	**23**	

OBSERVATIONS:

	ELECTIVE I	ELECTIVE II
VII SEMESTER:	Seed Technology	Small Bussiness Management
VIII SEMESTER:	Introduction to Computer Science	Introduction to Plant Breeding
IX SEMESTER:	Bee-Keeping	Fruit Crops II (Tropical)

PROMEDIOS / GRADE POINT AVERAGES

SEMESTER I :	3.09
SEMESTER II :	3.07
SEMESTER III :	2.63
SEMESTER IV :	2.44
SEMESTER V :	1.84
SEMESTER VI :	1.94
SEMESTER VII :	2.27
SEMESTER VIII :	2.39
SEMESTER IX :	2.82

PROMEDIO ACUMULATIVO / CUMULATIVE GRADE POINT AVERAGE: 2.49

NUMERO TOTAL DE CREDITOS / TOTAL CREDITS: 211

NUMERO DE ESTUDIANTES A LA GRADUACION / NUMBER OF STUDENTS AT GRADUATION: 161

POSICION DE ESTE ESTUDIANTE EN SU CLASE / POSITION OF THIS STUDENT FROM THE CLASS AT GRADUATION: 88th

CERTIFICADO CORRECTO / CERTIFIED CORRECT

REGISTRADOR / REGISTRAR

CERTIFICADO / CERTIFIED

DECANO / DEAN

Document 6.3 Students at the _Escuela Agrícola Panamericana/"Zamorano"_ (Pan American Agricultural School) take up to eight courses per semester, including field work.

Chapter 7
The Educational System of Nicaragua

The Country

Nicaragua underwent sweeping political changes in 1990, as the National Opposition Union (*UNO*) coalition came to power under the leadership of Violeta Chamorro. After defeating the Sandinista government, which had led Nicaragua through a decade of revolutionary change, a divisive and costly war, and an economic blockade, the UNO government has attempted to rebuild a working civil society in Nicaragua. While peace has arrived, and economic and political ties with the United States are restored, the government remains extremely unstable and the economic situation has not improved. The unemployment rate has been estimated at between 50-70 percent, and socio-economic indicators such as rates of malnutrition, crime, and drug abuse have remained high.

The Nicaraguan state universities are poorly funded and their facilities are in need of modernization. Political disagreements between the government and the univer-sities have also affected the quality of educational opportunities, as funding decisions and subsidies are influenced by the ongoing ideological polarization.

Reestablished Nicaraguan-U.S. relations and an end to the war have spurred many exiled Nicaraguans to return home, bringing with them in some cases an orientation toward the U.S. educational system. Several private universities have opened since the change in government, and there is a trend toward flexibility in programs of study (as opposed to the "block" system of requirements described below). These new universities also tend to offer programs in business administration, and technical skills such as computer sciences.

Postsecondary Education

There are ten universities in Nicaragua: the *Universidad Autónoma de Nicaragua/UNAN*, the *Universidad Autónoma de Nicaragua-León/UNAN-León*, the *Universidad Centroamericana/UCA*, the *Universidad de Ingeniería/UNI*, the *Universidad Nacional Agraria/UNA*, the

Official Name: Republic of Nicaragua

Area: 130,000 square km./50,000 square miles (slightly larger than New York State)

Capital: Managua

Population: 4 million

Annual growth rate: 3.4 percent

Noun and adjective: Nicaraguan(s)

Ethnic groups: Mestizo (indigenous and European descent) 69%; Caucasian 17%; Black 9%; indigenous (Miskito, Sumo, Rama) 5%

Languages: Primarily Spanish, (Also Miskito, Sumo, Rama, Garifuna)

Religion: Catholic, growing Protestant minority

Education: Years compulsory-11 years of school or 16 years old; Attendance -Primary school completion rate is 20%; Literacy-30-40%

(Source: U.S. State Department *Background Notes*)

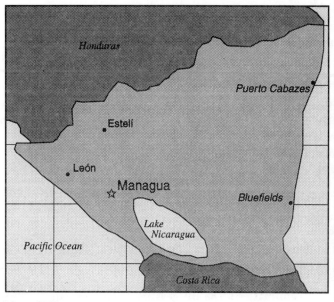

Map of Nicaragua

Universidad Politécnica/ UPOLI, the Universidad Católica/UNICA, the Bluefields Caribbean and Indian University/BICU, the Universidad Autónoma Americana/ UAM. The tenth institution, the Universidad de las Regiones Autónomas de la Costa Caribe de Nicaragua/ URACCAN, has recently opened.

At the undergraduate or pregrado level, Nicaraguan universities award the técnico, diplomado, licenciado, ingeniero, or professional título (title), which reflects the graduate's carrera (field of study or major). First degree programs for the ingeniero or licenciado vary in length from 4 to 5 years. Programs leading to professional titles are usually 5 years in length, with 6 years for medicine. Graduate programs (postgrado) are few, and are either maestría or postgrado degrees.

Most Nicaraguan universities function with a "block" system of course requirements. In this system, 4 to 7 specific courses are required for each 16-week block. Two blocks equal one academic year of 20-32 hours of weekly study. Students follow a fixed curriculum for the duration of the carrera. However, with the emergence of new universities and curricula, this traditional structure is undergoing some reforms and shows signs of offering more flexibility in the future.

From 1979 to 1990, the oversight body for approving universities and degree programs was the National Council for Higher Education (Consejo Nacional de Educación Superior or CNES). With the change of government in 1990, the National University Council (Consejo Nacional de Universidades or CNU) became the organization charged with this task. Its predecessor, CNES, no longer exists. The CNU has restored much of the autonomy that the universities had prior to 1979.

Grading System: Nicaraguan universities grade on a scale of 0 to 100 points. 60 is generally the minimum passing grade.

Institutional Profiles

Bluefields Indian and Caribbean University/ BICU
Apartado 88
Bluefields
Tel. 8222544

Established: June 6, 1991 and authorized by CNU to grant degrees: March 5, 1992

- **Academic calendar:** Two semesters, March to July and August to December

- **Organization:** The BICU is the "first university designed and directed by natives of the Atlantic Coast of Nicaragua to respond to the needs, aspirations, characteristics, and specific rights of the

autonomous regions and its multi-ethnic and multi-cultural inhabitants." Its future plans include programs in distance education to serve the residents of Nicaragua's Atlantic Coast. Although the region's primary language is English, instruction is in Spanish or taught bilingually.

The establishment of the BICU is a major development for the inhabitants of the Atlantic Coast, which has traditionally been economically, politically, and educationally isolated from the rest of Nicaragua. The city of Bluefields, where the university is located, was nearly devastated by a hurricane in 1989. Its 70,000 residents have historically had to travel to Managua or another part of the country for university studies; the arrival of the BICU should make a great impact on the educational demands of this community.

- **Credentials Awarded:** At this writing BICU has yet to graduate its first class. The programs marked with an asterisk (*) were scheduled to be offered during 1994, but it is too early to determine whether or not these carreras (majors) will all be offered for the duration of the 2.5-5 year period. (See Document 7.1)

Programs offered	Credential	Duration
Agroforestry and Fishery Sciences	licenciado	5 years
Civil Engineering	ingeniero	5 years
Civil Engineering and Construction	técnico superior	3 years
Education Sciences	licenciado	5 years
Fishery Business Administration	licenciado	4 years
Forestry	ingeniero	5 years
Humid Tropics Agronomy	técnico	3 years
Law	licenciado	5 years
Marine Biology	licenciado	5 years
Port Engineering	ingeniero	5 years
Professional Nursing	licenciado	5 years
Public Administration	técnico superior	2.5 years
Tropical Disease Medicine	doctor	5 years

Universidad Autónoma Americana/UAM
(American Autonomous University)
Reparto Bolonia
Club Terraza 20 mts. al Oeste
Frente a Oficinas OEA
PO Box A-139
Managua

Tel: 225589, 226743
Fax: 222834

Established in 1992, the UAM officially opened its door to 780 students in the fall of 1993. In 1994, it reported an enrollment of approximately 1,000. Unlike most Nicaraguan institutions, which operate on a "block" system of course offerings, the UAM offers a flexible program of required courses and electives.

The maximum number of credits in which a student may enroll is 18; the minimum is 6. All students are required to take an introductory computer course and a common core of courses during the first year. The undergraduate *licenciado* programs consist of 10 semesters (5 years) of study, but students may opt for a *diplomado* (intermediate) degree after completing 3 years at the university. Additionally, students who maintain a grade point average of at least 90% are permitted to enroll in extra credits and may complete *licenciado* degree programs in 4 years; 70% is the minimum passing grade.

Programs offered:	Credential:
Judicial and Philosophical Sciences:	
Law	*licenciado*
Political Science	*licenciado*
Diplomacy and	
International Relations	*licenciado*
Accounting and Administrative Sciences:	
Marketing	*licenciado*
Public Accounting	*licenciado*
Auditing	*licenciado*
School of Communications:	
Communications Science	*licenciado*
Advertising	*licenciado*
School of Technology	
Agricultural Engineering	*licenciado*
Computer Sciences	*licenciado*
Topography	*técnico superior*
Industrial Supervision	*técnico superior*
Humanities	
Psychology	*licenciado*
Anthropology	*licenciado*
Medical Sciences:	
Medicine	*doctor*
Dentistry	*doctor*
Medical Technology	*técnico superior*
Hygiene	*técnico superior*
Dental Assistance	*técnico superior*
Optometry	*técnico superior*

Universidad Católica "Redemptoris Mater"/ UNICA ("Redemptoris Mater" Catholic University)
Km. 9 1/2 Carretera a Masaya, 500 Varas al S.O.

Managua
Tel: 2760008, 2760004
Fax: 2760005

The *UNICA* was established in 1991 by Cardinal Miguel Obando y Bravo. In the the fall of 1993, there were approximately 1,700 students enrolled. The school planned to add degree programs in Optometry and Dentistry in 1995; plans are also underway for construction of a medical school and hospital.

Credentials Awarded: The university offers *licenciado* degrees in the following areas:

School of Business Administration:
  Banking and Commercial Administration
  Industrial Administration
  Agricultural Administration
  Marketing
  Public Administration

School of Engineering:
  Civil Engineering
  Industrial Engineering
  Mechanical Engineering
  Computer Engineering
  Architecture

Law

Social Sciences:
  History
  Geography
  Sociology
  Communications
  International Relations
  Psychology

School of Humanities:
  Philosophy
  Letters
  Theology

Universidad Centroamericana/UCA
(Central American University)
Apartado Postal 69
Managua
Tel: 2670352, 2670588, 2673871
Fax: 2670106

The *Universidad Centroamericana* is a private Jesuit university in Managua. It is the oldest and most prestigious private institution in the country, traditionally concentrating in the social and technological sciences.

Facilities: In addition to its 41,256 volume library, the *UCA* houses the *Instituto Historico Centroamericano* (Historic Central American Institute), which has approximately 20,000 volumes on Nicaragua. The university also has its own press, radio station, and a farm for students' practical experience in agriculture.

- **Grading Scale:** 1-10; since 1970 minimum passing grade has been 6. (The minimum passing grade prior to 1970 was 5).

Program offered	Credential	Duration (years)
Administrative Sciences		
Business administration	*licenciado*	5 (daytime), 6 (evening)
Agricultural Sciences		
Agricultural administration	*licenciado*	5
Animal Science	*licenciado*	5
Nutrition	*licenciado*	5
Ecology and Natural Resources	*licenciado*	5
Foreign Languages		
English Translation	*licenciado*	5
Russian Translation	*licenciado*	
Humanities		
Arts and Letters	*licenciado*	5*
Journalism	*licenciado*	5
Library Science	*licenciado*	5
Psychology	*licenciado*	5
Social Work	*licenciado*	5
Sociology	*licenciado*	5
Legal and Social Sciences		
Law	*licenciado*	5 (daytime), 6 (evening)

*(See Document 7.2)

Instituto de Comercio Exterior y Gerencia Empresarial/INCEG (Institute of Foreign Trade and Business Management)
Apartado 68
Managua

Recinto Universitario Ricardo Morales Aviles Semáforos I.N.E.
Central 500 metros al sur
Managua
Tel: 73699, 75623
Fax: 75623

Universidad de las Regiones Autónomas de la Costa Caribe de Nicaragua/URACCAN
(University of the Autonomous Regions of the Caribbean Coast of Nicaragua)
Paseo Tiscapa
Busto José Martí, 1/2 cuadra arriba
Contiguo a Editorial Vanguardia
Apartado Postal 891
Managua
Tel.: 621112
Fax: 226977

URACCAN opened in 1995 as the second university on the Atlantic Coast. It will have three branches: Bluefields, Puerto Cabezas, and Siuna, each of which serves approximately 150 students per year. Anticipated courses of study are fisheries, forestry, mining, nursing, sociology of autonomy, and education (principally teacher training.)

Universidad Nacional Agraria/UNA **(National Agrarian University)**
(formerly *Instituto Superior de Ciencias Agropecuarias/ISCA*, **and** *Escuela Nacional de Agricultura y Ganadería/ENAG*, **and Agriculture College of the** *UNAN*)
Km 12 1/2 Carretera Norte
Apartado Postal: 453
Managua
Tel: 2331473
Fax: 2331950

In 1917, a Technical School of Agriculture was established in the city of Chinandega. In 1929, the *Escuela Nacional de Agricultura y Ganadería/ENAG*, was founded. In 1956, *ENAG* initiated a degree program in Agronomic Engineering. After fifty years, in 1979 *ENAG* was converted into the College (*Facultad*) of Agricultural and Livestock Sciences of the *Universidad Nacional Autónoma de Nicaragua/UNAN* in Managua.

In 1986, the college was converted into the *Instituto Superior de Ciencias Agrícolas/ISCA*. In 1990, with the implementation of the Law of Autonomy for Institutions of Higher Education, *ISCA* became the National Agricultural University/*UNA*.

- **Organization:** *UNA* has four colleges (*facultades*): Agronomy, Animal Sciences, Natural Resources and Environment, Rural Development and Distance Education. It has three farms for agricultural production, 25 laboratories, classrooms, computer facilities, dining rooms, sports accommodations, and dormitories for the students. The library is the National Center for Agricultural/Livestock Documentation and Information (*CENIDA*), which has over 12,500 volumes.

- **Faculty:** The university has 141 faculty members, and 238 administrators.

- **Enrollment:** 2,170 students.

Programs offered	Credential	Duration
Crop Protection	*ingeniero agrónomo*	5 years
Animal Sciences	*ingeniero agrónomo*	5 years
Soils and Water	*ingeniero agrónomo*	5 years
Crop Production	*ingeniero agrónomo*	5 years
Forestry Engineer	*ingeniero agrónomo*	5 years
Agronomist	*ingeniero agrónomo*	6 years*
Agricultural Education	*licenciado*	5 years
Rural Extension	*licenciado*	5 years**

*(part-time)
**(initiated in 1994)

Universidad Nacional Autónoma de Nicaragua -León/UNAN-León (National Autonomous University of Nicaragua-León)
Rectorado de UNAN-León
León
Tel: 3115731
Fax: 3114970

The *UNAN-León* traces its roots back to a Spanish seminary, founded in the city of León in 1670. It became the Universidad de León in 1812, and was granted autonomous status in 1958. Nicaragua's entire public university system in Nicaragua had its beginnings at this institution. *UNAN-Managua* was granted autonomy from León in 1982; the remaining branches are now affiliated with the capital city's campus.

- **Organization:** *UNAN-León* is divided into six faculties (*facultades*), as follows: 1. Chemical Sciences, 2. Dentistry, 3. Education, 4. Legal and Social Sciences, 5. Medical Sciences, 6. Sciences. New majors (*carreras*) that have emerged since 1990 are listed below:

Programs offered	Credential
Statistics-Computation	*técnico superior*
Education, with mention in:	*licenciado*
English	
Social Sciences	
Physics/Mathematics	
Chemistry/Biology	
Spanish	
Public Law	*maestría*
Analytic Chemistry	*maestría*
Statistics/Operations Research	*maestría*
Applied Physics	*maestría*
Pedagogy/ Teacher Training, with emphasis in morphology	*maestría*
Pest Control	*maestría*

Uiversidad Nacional Autónoma de Nicaragua/ UNAN (National Autonomous University of Nicaragua)
Recinto Universitario "Rubén Dario"
Del Instituto Nicaragüense de Energía (INE)
2.5 Kms. al Sur
Apartado 663
Managua
Tel: 2770064, 2773408
Fax: 2774943

Previously part of the *UNAN* system, including *UNAN-Leon*, it became an autonomous institution in 1982.

Academic calendar: March to January

Faculty: 877 (498 fulltime)

Enrollment: 13,357

- **Organization:** The *UNAN* is the oldest and largest public university system in Nicaragua. The university offers 43 academic programs, and between 1982 and 1993, the *UNAN* awarded 5,997 degrees to students. *UNAN* grants three degrees: *técnico superior* (3 years), *licenciado* (4-6 years), *licenciado superior* (6 years), and *doctor en medicina* (6 years).

Centro Universitario de la Región Autónoma del Atlántico Norte/CURAAN (University Center of the Autonomous North Atlantic Coast Region), Puerto Cabezas

The branch campus of *UNAN* in Puerto Cabezas, located in the northern Atlantic Coast region, has a student population of 164. It offers a postsecondary program in general studies.

Universidad Nacional de Ingeniería "Simón Bolívar"/UNI ("Simón Bolivar" National Engineering University)
Recinto Universitario Simon Bolívar
Apartado 5595
Pista de la Resistencia
Managua
Tel.: 26670274-77
Fax: 26673709
E-mail: rectoria@uni.ni

Recinto Universitario Pedro Arauz Palacios
Costado Sur de Villa Progreso
Managua
Tels.: 44257, 44287

The *UNI* was established in 1983 as an amalgamation of the engineering faculties from the *UCA* and *UNAN*.

- **Enrollment:** 6,542

- **Founded:** 1983

- **Grading system:** 0 to 100; minimum passing grade is 60%.

Programs offered	Credential	Duration
Agricultural Engineering	*ingeniero*	5 years
Architecture	*arquitecto*	5.5 years
Chemical Engineering	*ingeniero*	5 years
Civil Engineering	*ingeniero*	5 years
Computer Science	*ingeniero*	5.5 years
Industrial Engineering	*ingeniero*	5 years
Mechanical Engineering	*ingeniero*	5 years
Electronic Engineering	*ingeniero*	5 years
Electrical Engineering	*ingeniero*	5 years

In addition, the UNI offers a graduate (*maestría*) program in the environmental sciences called *Programa de Investigación y Docencia del Medio Ambiente* (Program of Research and Teaching of the Environment), known by its acronym, *PIDMA*. PIDMA offers 2-year master's (*maestría*) level programs in Environmental Engineering and in Environmental Sciences. Operating with a system of credits weighted for each course, the master's programs consist of 62 credits taken in 5 trimesters, plus an additional 3 trimesters for research and thesis writing.

Universidad Nacional de Ingeniería "Simón Bolívar"/UNI
("Simón Bolivar" National Engineering University: PIDMA Program)

Environmental Engineering		Environmental Sciences	
I. Trimester	**Credits**	**I. Trimester**	**Credits**
Applied Statistics	3	Applied Statistics	3
Environmental Chemistry	3	Environmental Chemistry	3
Microbiology	3	Microbiology	3
Hygiene, Epidemiology, Public Health	4	Hygiene, Epidemiology, Public Health	4
II. Trimester		**II. Trimester**	
Hydrology I	4	Hydrology I	4
Ecology	2	Ecology	2
*Environmental Pollution	4	Environmental (Saneamiento)	4
Project Formulation and Evaluation	3	Project Formulation and Evaluation	3
III. Trimester		**III. Trimester**	
*Hydrology II	4	Air and Soil Pollution	4
Solid Wastes	3	Limnology	2
*Water Impulsion and Distribution	4	Toxicology	3
Research Protocol	1	Research Protocol	1
		Natural Resources I	3
Environmental Engineering		Environmental Sciences	
IV. Trimester		**IV. Trimester**	
*Drainage Systems	4	Water Pollution	3
Unit Operations	4	Natural Resources II	3
Environmental Impact Evaluation	4	Environmental Impact Evaluation	4
Thesis Preparation I	1	Thesis Preparation I	1

V. Trimester			V. Trimester	
Purifying Plants	4		Ecotoxicology	4
Residual Water Treatments	3		Urban and Territorial Planning	4
*Rural Hygiene (Saneamiento)	3		Environmental Legislation	3
Thesis Preparation II	1		Thesis Preparation II	1
Total	62		Total	62

* Optional Courses
Mass Transfer, Air and Soil Pollution, Water Pollution, Ecotoxicology, and Numerical Methods

Universidad Politécnica de Nicaragua/UPOLI (Polytechnic University of Nicaragua)
Apartado 3595
Managua
Tel: 2897740-43
Fax: 2897659

UPOLI was established in 1967 by the Baptist church. Students are required to spend 5 weeks each year working as interns in their field of study. Admissions requirements include a *"Diploma de Bachillerato"* or *"Diploma de Técnico Medio;"* some majors also demand that candidates pass an admissions exam. The *licenciado* degree requires a thesis or monograph. The *UPOLI* offers majors in the following technical fields to approximately 1,700 students.

Programs offered	Credential	Duration:
School of Administration, Commerce, & Finance:		
Business		
Administration	*técnico superior**	3.5 yrs
	licenciado	*téc.* +2
Marketing	*técnico superior*	
	licenciado	
Banking and Finance	*técnico superior*	3 years (days) 3.5 years (evening)
	licenciado	*téc.* + 2 (days)

		téc.+ 2.5 (evening)
Agricultural Admin.	*técnico superior*	3 years (days)
School of Design:		
Industrial Design	*técnico superior* *licenciado*	
Graphic Design	*técnico superior* *licenciado*	3.5 years *téc.* +2.5
Statistics:		
Economic Statistics	*técnico superior* *licenciado*	3.5 years *téc.* +2.5
Nursing School:		
Nursing	*técnico superior* *licenciado*	2 years
Other:		
Computer Sciences†	*técnico superior*	3 years

* Generally written as simply *técnico* on most documents. (See Document 7.3)
† This new program is offered through the Computer Sciences Institute (ICC), which is affiliated with the UPOLI.

Other postsecondary institutions

There are several university programs offered in Nicaragua which are run by foreign entities. The oldest of these is *INCAE*, the *Instituto Centroamericano de Administración de Empresas* (Central American Institute of Business Administration). *INCAE* in Managua is a branch of the Costa Rican-based graduate school offering master's degrees in business-related fields of study (see Costa Rica chapter for more information).

Glossary

Abogado(a). Lawyer

Aplazado. Failed

Arquitecto(a). Architect

Bachillerato or *bachiller.* Secondary school diploma.

Carrera. Program of study/major/specialization

Cirujano Dentista. Dental Surgeon

Doctor/Doctorado. Doctor, usually of medicine or dentistry (a first university degree in Nicaragua); also may be a graduate level doctorate in philosophy, a credential that is emerging in Central American higher education.

Especialización. Specialization

Ingeniero(a)/Ingeniería. Engineer(ing)

Licenciado(a)/Licenciatura. Licentiate, generally first university degree

Materia de Arrastre. Make-up course

Maestría. Master's

Maestro/a. Teacher

Pensum. List of required courses and prerequisites for a specific program; also called *plan de estudios* (study plan)

Perito. Expert

Práctica. Practicum or internship, required for some programs

Profesorado. Teaching degree

Profesor(a) en (specialization). Teacher of (specialization)

Técnico en. (specialization) Technician in (specialization)

Técnico Superior. Higher technician

Título. Title/ degree

Document 7.1 Cover of the Bluefields Indian and Caribbean University/BICU catalog, reflecting the bilingual flavor of the Atlantic Coast

UNIVERSIDAD CENTROAMERICANA   0438-93

FACULTAD DE: HUMANIDADES

ESCUELA DE: ARTE Y LETRAS

Managua, D. N., Nicaragua.

REGISTRO INDIVIDUAL

Fecha de nacimiento: 09 MAYO 1966

Lugar de nacimiento: Rivas, Rivas.

NOMBRE DEL ALUMNO:

ELIZABETH

No. de Registro:

República de Nicaragua.

Fecha de ingreso: 1990

No. del curso	NOMBRE DEL CURSO	Creditos.	Primera Convocatoria		Segunda Convocatoria		Puntos
			Nota	Acta	Nota	Acta	
	I AÑO I SEMESTRE 1990						
0101	Español I		67	SESENTA Y SIETE			18124
0102	Filosofía Introductoria		63	SESENTA Y TRES			
0103	Historia Revolución Popular Sandinista		62	SESENTA Y DOS			
0104	Antropología Cultural		74	SETENTA Y CUATRO			
	I AÑO II SEMESTRE 1990						
0201	Español II		59	CINCUENTA Y NUEVE			18191
0205	Sociología Introductoria		69	SESENTA Y NUEVE			
0206	Teoría Literaria		92	NOVENTA Y DOS			
0207	Cultura Nacional		60	SESENTA			
	II AÑO III SEMESTRE 1991						
0301	Historia Antigua y Media		90	NOVENTA			18351
0302	Psicología General		67	SESENTA Y SIETE			
0303	Literatura Universal I		81	OCHENTA Y UNO			
0304	Teoría del Arte		88	OCHENTA Y OCHO			
	II AÑO IV SEMESTRE 1991						
0401	Literatura Universal II		100	CIEN			18369
0402	Historia Moderna y Contemporanea		80	OCHENTA			
0403	Teoría de la Enseñanza		78	SETENTA Y OCHO			
0404	Teoría del Cine		88	OCHENTA Y OCHO			
0201	Español II		78	SETENTA Y OCHO			18386
	III AÑO V SEMESTRE 1992						
0503	Historia Evolutiva del Teatro		91	NOVENTA Y UNO			
0504	Historia del Arte I		89	OCHENTA Y NUEVE			
0505	Idioma Extranjero I		100	CIEN			
0506	Literatura Contemporanea I		87	OCHENTA Y SIETE			
	III AÑO VI SEMESTRE 1992						
0602	Historia del Arte II		84	OCHENTA Y CUATRO			
0603	Teflexión Teológica		82	OCHENTA Y DOS			
0604	Teatro Contemporaneo		84	OCHENTA Y CUATRO			
0605	Idioma Extranjero II		92	NOVENTA Y DOS			
0606	Literatura Contemporanea II		89	OCHENTA Y NUEVE			

Dado en Managua, D.N., Nicaragua, a los ___Doce___ días

del mes de ___Mayo___ de 19 __93.__   Recibo # _____ - 187288

(No es válido si no está acompañado de la "Definición de Notas", sellada).

Document 7.2 Partial *Universidad Centroamericana/UCA* **(Central American University) transcript**

EN CORDOBA ORO

Nº 0000000

C E R T I F I C A C I O N

La Suscrita Directora del Departamento de Admisión y Registro -

de la Universidad Politécnica de Nicaragua, CERTIFICA. Que de acuerdo

Con los Registros Académicos que este Departamento lleva, _____

LLA, cursó y aprobó las materias que se detallan a continuación Correspondientes a la

Carrera TECNICO EN MERCADEO, que ofrece esta Universidad habiendo obtenido las Siguien-

tes Calificaciones:

SIMBOLO:	NOMBRE DE LA MATERIA:	CALIFICACION:
	SEMESTRE: MARZO * JULIO * 1990* I AÑO	
MBG-19	Historia de la Rev. Pop. Sandinista	94.- Sobresal.
MBG-12	Matemática Básica	62.- Aprobado
MBG-02	Español	81.- Muy Bueno
TBF-03	Introducción al Estudio del Derecho	86.- Muy Bueno
TMC-02	Relaciones Humanas y Comunicación	84.- Muy Bueno
TBF-04	Contabilidad I	77.- Bueno
TMC-01	Administración I	72.- Bueno
	SEMESTRE: AGOSTO * NOVIEMBRE* 1990* I AÑO	
TBF-05	Contabilidad II	89.- Muy Bueno
TBF-10	Administración II	61.- Aprobado
TBF-13 *	Matemática I	46.- Aplazado
TMC-03	Principios de Mercadeo	93.- Sobresal.
TMC-07	Idioma Extranjero I	98.- Sobresal.
TBF-01	Economía I	83.- Muy Bueno
TBF-16	Estadística I	82.- Muy Bueno
	EXAMEN ESPECIAL:	
TBF-13 *	Matemática I	20.- Aplazado
	SEMESTRE: MARZO * JULIO * 1991* II AÑO	
TMC-08	Idioma Extranjero II	96.- Sobresal.
TMC-09	Economía II	83.- Muy Bueno

Document 7.3a A 3-year *técnico* at the *Universidad Politécnica de Nicaragua/UPOLI* (Poly-technic University of Nicaragua). Student was given three chances to pass Mathematics I.

SIMBOLO:	NOMBRE DE LA MATERIA:	CALIFICACION:
TBF-14	Matemática Financiera I	74.- Bueno
TMC-04	Mercadotecnia I	90.- Sobresal.
TBF-08	Derecho Mercantil	80.- Muy Bueno
TMC-11	Ventas I	81.- Muy Bueno

SEMESTRE: AGOSTO * NOVIEMBRE* 1991* II AÑO

TBF-15	Matemática Financiera II	79.- Bueno
TMC-05	Mercadotecnia II	71.- Bueno
TMC-12	Ventas II	77.- Bueno
TMC-13b	Técnicas de Investigación	78.- Bueno
TBF-25	Finanzas I	71.- Bueno
TMC-14	Producción	71.- Bueno

MATERIA DE ARRASTRE:

TBF-13	Matemática I	95.- Sobresal.

SEMESTRE: MARZO * AGOSTO * 1992* III AÑO

TMC-06	Mercadotecnia III	71.- Bueno
TMC-10	Economía de la Empresa	72.- Bueno

SEMESTRE: SEPT. 1992* ENERO* 1993* III AÑO

TBF-25	Finanzas II	79.- Bueno
TDP-06	Publicidad	80.- Muy Bueno
TMC-15	Promoción Exterior	78.- Bueno
TMC-16	Investigación de Mercados	69.- Aprobado

La escala de Calificación es del 0 al 100, siendo 60 la nota mínima para aprobar. Es conforme a su original con el cual fue debidamente cotejado y a solicitud del intere-sado, extiendo la presente CERTIFICACION en la Ciudad de Managua a los siete días del mes de Mayo de mil novecientos noventa y tres.

MAYRA RODRIGO GARC.
DIRECTO...

Document 7.3b (see previous)

Chapter 8
The Educational System of Panama

The Country

Panama has traditionally maintained close ties to the United States, primarily due to U.S. control of the canal, which is to be turned over to Panama at the end of the decade. Panama's economy is dominated by a large service sector, with approximately 79% of Gross Domestic Product (GDP) dedicated to banking, insurance, and canal-related services. This emphasis is reflected throughout secondary and postsecondary curricula, where there is a strong emphasis on computer education, engineering, technical areas, and mathematics. The public *Universidad Tecnológica* has an enrollment of nearly 10,000 students, and there are today numerous computer-training institutes located throughout the country.

The December 1989 U.S. military intervention in Panama resulted in bringing to power President Guillermo Endara of the Arnulfista Party. In 1994 President Endara was succeeded by Ernesto Pérez Balladares of the Revolutionary Democratic Party (PRD), the party of General Omar Torrijos.

The People

Like other Caribbean nations, Panama has a mixture of mestizos (mixed Spanish and indigenous blood), indigenous groups such as the Cuna, Guaymi, and Embera or Choco, West Indian, and Chinese inhabitants. While the majority of the population speaks Spanish, English and a Creole dialect are also heard in parts of the country. English acquisition is further assisted by the presence of the U.S. Southern Command, which runs an AM/FM radio transmitter and a television station.

There is a great deal of interest in Panama today in reviving its traditions and educating inhabitants about the nation's indigenous population. Protecting the environment and preserving natural resources have become a preoccupation for both the government, social groups, and the schools.

Official name: Republic of Panama

Area: 77,381 square kilometers/29,762 square miles (about the size of South Carolina)

Capital: Panama City

Population: 2.4 million

Annual growth rate: 2.5 percent

Noun and adjective: Panamanian(s)

Ethnic groups: Mestizo 70%; West Indian 14%, white 10%, indigenous 6%

Religions: Catholic, Protestant minority (approximately 6%)

Languages: Spanish (official), 14% speak English as their native tongue; various indigenous languages.

Education: Years compulsory-6; Attendance-95%; Literacy-87% overall, 94% urban, 62% rural.

(Source: U.S. State Department *Background Notes*)

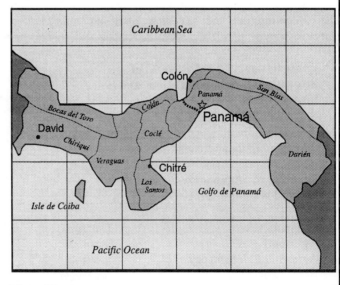

Map of Panama

Postsecondary Education

Postsecondary education in Panama has traditionally been concentrated at two public institutions, the *Universidad de Panama* and the *Universidad Tecnológica de Panama*, and at the private Catholic *Universidad Santa María la Antigua/USMA*. Non-university programs are also offered at *escuelas* and *institutos*, including the *Escuela Naútica de Panama*, which offers a 5-year program in Maritime Engineering, the *Instituto Superior de Turismo* (Higher Institute of Tourism), and the *Instituto Superior de Enseñanza*, which trains teachers for the disabled.

There are also several new universities, such as the *Universidad Interamericana de Educación a Distancia de Panama*, Columbus University, the *Universidad Latinoamericana de Ciencia y Tecnología*, and the *Universidad Latina*. The latter two institutions are branches of Costa Rican private universities. Given the regional trend toward privatization in higher education, more private universities and other postsecondary programs can be expected to emerge in the coming years. Finally, the Panama Canal College and Florida State University's Panama branch complete the spectrum of Panama's postsecondary educational options.

Credentials Awarded

The *bachiller* is required for admission into postsecondary institutions. Postsecondary credentials offered in Panama are:

Credential	Translation	Prerequisite	Duration
Técnico en (specialization)	Technician in	*bachiller* *	1-3 years
Profesor en educación primaria	Primary School Teacher	*bachiller*	3 years
Licenciado/Título Profesional	Licentiate/Professional Degree	*bachiller*	4-6 years
Doctor en Cirugía Dental	Dental Surgeon	*bachiller*	5 years
Doctor en Medicina	Medical Doctor	*bachiller*	6 years
Maestría	Masters	*licenciado*	2 years + thesis
Doctor	Doctorate	*licenciado*	3 years, exam, thesis

* Secondary school degree
(Source: World Education *News & Reviews*, Vol. 7, No. 1, Winter 1993)

Institutional Profiles

***Universidad de Panama/UP* (University of Panama)**
Estafeta Universitaria
Panama 3
Panama
Tel: 63-61-33

The following are the faculties, institutes, and programs of study at the *Universidad de Panama:*

Central American Institute of Educational Administration and Supervision

Programs offered	Credential
Educational Administration	*maestría*

Faculty of Agronomy
Founded November 20, 1959

Programs offered	Credential
Agronomy	*ingeniero*
Agricultural Entomology	*maestría*
Home Economics	*licenciado*

Faculty of Architecture
Founded May 18, 1962
(Preceded by the School of Engineering and Architecture, founded in 1943).

Programs offered	Credential
Architectural Drawing	*técnico*
Architecture	*licenciado*
Applied Arts Design	*licenciado*
Applied Arts Design	*técnico*
Graphic Design	*licenciado*
Interior Design	*licenciado*
Interior Design	*técnico*

Faculty of Business Administration and Accounting
Founded June 25, 1982

Programs offered	Credential
Accounting	*licenciado*
Business Administration	*licenciado*
International Trade	*programa de especialización*
Spanish and English Executive Secretary	*secretariado ejecutivo*

Faculty of Dentistry
Founded October 7, 1967

Faculty of Economics
Founded March 25, 1982

Program offered	Credential
Economics	*licenciado*

Faculty of Education
Founded July 9, 1965

Programs offered	Credential
Education	*licenciado*
Education	*profesorado*
Preschool Education	*profesorado*
Primary Education	*profesorado*
Higher Education Teaching	*programa de especialización*

Profesorado degrees are also offered at other UP schools, depending on the academic area in which the student plans to teach.

Faculty of Humanities (Philosophy, Letters and Education)
Founded October 7, 1935

Programs offered	Credential
Library Science	*técnico*
English	*licenciado*
French	*licenciado*
Geography	*licenciado*
Geography and History	*licenciado*
Library Science	*licenciado*
Meteorology	*técnico*
Music	*licenciado*
Philosophy and History	*licenciado*
Physical Education	*licenciado*
Psychology	*licenciado*
Sociology	*licenciado*
Spanish	*licenciado*

Faculty of Law and Political Science
Founded May 30, 1935
Preceded by the National Law Faculty, founded January 25, 1918

Program offered	Credential
Law and Political Science	*licenciado*

Faculty of Medicine
Founded May 21, 1951

Programs offered	Credential
Medical Entomology	*maestría*
Medicine	*doctor*
Public Health	*maestría*

Faculty of Natural and Exact Sciences
Founded October 7, 1935

Programs offered	Credential
Biology	*licenciado*
Chemistry	*licenciado*
Mathematics	*licenciado*
Mathematics	*maestría*
Physics	*licenciado*
Statistics	*licenciado*

Faculty of Nursing
Founded January 29, 1985

Programs offered	Credential
Nursing Sciences	*licenciado*
Nursing Services Admin.	*curso postbásico*
Maternal-Infant Nursing	*curso postbásico*
Maternal-Infant Nursing	*maestría*
Pediatric Nursing	*curso postbásico*
Community Health Nursing	*curso postbásico*
Mental Health and Psychiatry	*curso postbásico*

Faculty of Public Administration
Founded May 25, 1982

Programs offered	Credential
Customs Administration	*técnico*
Executive Secretary	*secretariado ejecutivo*
International Relations	*licenciado*
Public Administration	*licenciado*
Public Management	*programa de especialización*
Social Work	*licenciado*

Faculty of Social Communication
Founded June 13, 1984

Programs offered	Credential
Advertising	*licenciado*
Journalism	*licenciado*
Public Relations	*licenciado*
Radio Communications	*licenciado*

School of Pharmacy
Founded April 28, 1920

Program offered	Credential
Pharmacy	*licenciado*

University of Panama Branches

Centro Regional Universitario de Azuero
(Regional University Center of Azuero)
Founded: January 7, 1970

Centro Regional Universitario de Coclé
(Regional University Center of Cocle)
Founded: June 5, 1965

Centro Regional Universitario de Colón
(Regional University Center of Colón)
Founded: December 11, 1961

Centro Regional Universitario de Chiriquí (Regional University Center of Chiriquí)
Founded: September 7, 1974

Centro Regional Universitario de Los Santos (Regional University Center of Los Santos)
Founded: October 23, 1986

Centro Regional Universitario de Veraguas (Regional University Center of Veraguas)
Founded: January 13, 1958

"Popular Universities"

The "Popular" Universities (*universidades populares*) are regional extension branches.

Universidad Popular de Azuero
Founded: June 5, 1974

Universidad Popular de Coclé
Founded: August 30, 1973

Universidad Popular del Darien
Founded: April 16, 1980

Grading System:

A	*Sobresaliente*	(Excellent)
B	*Bueno*	(Good)
C	*Regular*	(Average)
D	*Deficiente*	(Poor, but passing)
F	*Fracasado*	(Failing)

Classes operate on a semester system. Each semester lasts 18 weeks, and each class meets for 45 minutes.

Plan of Study, College of Social Communication, School of Journalism, *Licenciado* in Journalism

Course (First Year)	Number of Semesters	Annual Credits
Introduction to Logic and Scientific Method	2	6
Sociology of Communication	2	6
General English	2	6
Introduction to Communication	2	6
History of U.S.- Panamanian Relations	2	6
Introduction to Journalism and Journalism in Panama	2	6
Language of Communication	2	6
Total		42

Course (Second Year)	Number of Semesters	Annual Credits
Information Techniques	2	6
Social Psychology	2	6
Political and Economic Geography	2	6
Journalistic Photography	1	3
Research Methodology	2	6
Communication Theory	2	6
General English I	2	6
Electives (One Required):		
Universal Literature	1	
French for Journalism	1	
Human Relations	1	3
Total		42

Course (Third Year)	Number of Semesters	Annual Credits
Information Technique II	2	6
Radio and Audiovisual Journalism	2	6
Public Opinion	2	6
Specialized Journalism I (Sports, Agriculture, Law, Economics)	2	6
Special English II	1	3
Propaganda (News)	1	3
Diagramming	2	6
Literature and Journalism Electives (One Required)		
Contemporary Political Thought	1	
Semantics	1	
Principles of Economics	1	3
Seminars (Required)		
Ecology and Environment		2
Human Rights	1	2
Total		46

Course (Fourth Year)	Number of Semesters	Annual Credits
Information Technique III	2	6
Specialized Journalism	2	6
Journalistic Ethics and Legislation	2	6
Interpretive and Opinion Journalism	2	6
Professional Practicum	2	6
Degree Work	2	6

Seminars (One Required During Final Semester)

New International Informational Order	1	
Alternative Journalism	1	
Journalistic Perspectives and Tendencies	1	
Cinematographic Appreciation and Analysis	1	
Government Structure	1	3
Total		39

Total hours required for graduation: 207
Total credits required for graduation: 169

Columbus University
Via España y Vía Brasil
Frente al Super Mercado GAGO
Panama City
Tel.: 63-3888
Fax: 63-3896

Authorized to grant degrees: February 25, 1994. Classes are offered mornings, afternoons, evenings, and weekends.

Programs offered	Credential
Law and Political Science	
International Relations	*licenciado*
Law and Political Science	*licenciado*
International Public Law	*maestría*
Criminal Law	*maestría*
Administrative Law	*maestría*
Political Science	*maestría*
Information and Social Sciences	
Information Sciences	*licenciado*
Sociology	*licenciado*
Psychology	*licenciado*
Social and Community Work	*licenciado*
Protocol and Public Relations	*licenciado*
Experimental Social Psychology	*maestría*

Programs offered	Credential
Commercial Sciences	
Accounting and Auditing	*licenciado*
Executive Secretary and Computers-Spanish	*licenciado*
Executive Secretary and Computers-Bilingual	*licenciado*
Office Administration and Secretarial Affairs	*licenciado*
Publicity and Marketing	*licenciado*
Accounting and Comptroller	*maestría*
Publicity and Marketing	*maestría*
Natural, Medical and Technological Sciences	
Medicine and Surgery	*licenciado*
Systems Engineering and Administration	*licenciado*
Mechanical and Naval Machinery Engineering	*licenciado*
Electronic Engineering and Communications	*licenciado*
Architecture and Structural Systems	*licenciado*
Statistics and Computer Science	*licenciado*
Statistics and Computer Science	*maestría*
Nautical Engineering and Maritime Transportation	*licenciado*
Civil Engineering and Structural Analysis	*licenciado*
Engineering and Industrial Administration	*licenciado*
Engineering and Industrial Administration	*maestría*
Education and Linguistics	
Secondary Teaching	*profesorado**
English Language	*licenciado*
Pre-School Education	*licenciado*
Primary School Education	*licenciado*
Educational Planning and Administration	*maestría*
Higher Education Teaching	*maestría*
Didactic Sciences	*maestría*
Linguistics	*maestría*
English Literature	*maestría*

* Area of academic specialization must be indicated.

Programs offered	Credential
Administrative and Economic Sciences	
Administration and Management	*licenciado*
Administration and Management	*maestría*
Administration and Human Resources	*licenciado*
Administration and Human Resources	*maestría*

Programs offered	Credential
Administration and Tourism	
Businesses	*licenciado*
Economics	*licenciado*
Finance, Securities, and Banking	*licenciado*
Finance, Securities, and Banking	*licenciado*
Economics Engineering	*maestría*

Instituto Superior de Especialización/ISE
(Higher Institute of Specialization)

The *Instituto Superior de Especialización/ISE* is part of the larger *Instituto Panameño de Habilitación Especial/IPHE*, a national organization that has served the nation's needs in special education since its foundation in 1951. *ISE* is a postsecondary institution, founded by *IPHE* in 1969, which operates from *IPHE*'s headquarters and also through a distance education program to reach the country's interior. Since 1979, *ISE* has trained teachers in a program called *docente integral* (integral teacher), which offers specializations in education of the deaf, blind, and mentally retarded. It has 22 faculty members and an administrative staff.

A state-run program that trains teachers in special education and serves more than 7,000 Panamanians,. *IPHE* currently has 1,047 employees in 16 centers.

Universidad Interamericana de Educación a Distancia de Panama/UNIEDPA
(Interamerican Distance Education University of Panama)
Calle 45 este y Ave. 5o
Bella Vista
Apdo. 6-10119
Panama City
Tel: 64-4633
Fax: 64-4655

- **Established:** 1986; Authorized to grant degrees: March 19, 1986

- **Enrollment**: 415

- **Faculty:** 71

- **Credentials Awarded:** The *UNIEDPA* grants the following degrees: *técnico universitario, licenciado, profesorado, maestría,* and *doctorado*. *Licenciado* programs are generally 4 years in duration, and they consist of 1 year of General Culture (*Cultura General*), 2 years of an "Integral" Curriculum (*Ciclo Integral*), after which the *técnico universitario* degree may be awarded, and a fourth year for specialized studies. With a fifth year added, the *profesorado* degree is awarded. *Maestría*

programs consist of 3 semesters plus a thesis, and candidates must possess a *licenciado* degree to qualify for admission. After completing the *maestría*, students may qualify for a *doctorado* with 2 additional years of study and a thesis.

- **Grading System**: Five point scale (1.0 to 5.0); 3.5 is the minimum passing grade and the cumulative average required for graduation.

The university has branches in Veraguas, Chiriquí, and Chitré.

Programs offered	Credential
Administration and Accounting	
Business Administration	*licenciado*
Accounting	*licenciado*
Marketing	*licenciado*
Foreign Trade	*licenciado*
Personnel Administration	*licenciado*
Financial Administration	
and Banking	*licenciado*
Education	
Education Science	*licenciado*
Pre-School Education	*licenciado*
Primary School Education	*licenciado*
Adult Education	*licenciado*
Psychopedagogy	*licenciado*
University Teaching	*maestría*
Higher Education Planning	
and Administration	*maestría*
Adult Education	*doctorado*
Education	*doctorado*
Law and Political Science	*licenciado**
Secretarial Administration	*licenciado*
	técnico universitario
Tourism Guide	*técnico universitario*

* Note: This *licenciado* requires five years of study.

Universidad Latina (Latin University)
Apartado 870887
Panama City, Zona 7

- **Established:** September 4, 1991

- **Organization:** The *Universidad Latina* (or *Univer-sidad Latina de Costa Rica,* as it is commonly known), is the sister institution of the *Universidad Latina in Costa Rica*. Its intermediate and *licenciado* degrees are offered in quarters (*cuatrimestres*) of 15 weeks; class periods last 55 minutes. Most plans of study require that students enroll in four courses per quarter; a *licenciado* degree requires 11 *cuatrimestres* for graduation. In addition to the *licenciado*, the university offers a *bachillerato* program. The *bachillerato* in Administration, for example, consists of 8 *cuatrimestres* of study. If students continue for an additional 4 quarters, the *licenciado* is awarded. (See Document 8.1)

- **Grading system:**

90-100	Excellent (*sobresaliente*)
80-90	Good (*bueno*)
70-80	Average (*regular*)
60-70	Passing (*mínima de promoción*)
0-60	Failing (*fracaso*)

Universidad Latinoamericana de Ciencia y Tecnología/ULACIT (Latin American Science and Technology University)
Tel: 64-9167/64-9624
Fax: 23-2732
Founded: July 1991.

The sister university of *ULACIT* in Costa Rica, *ULACIT* is a private postsecondary institution in Panama.

Universidad Santa María La Antigua/USMA (Santa Maria La Antigua University)
Apartado 6-1696
El Dorado, Panama
Tel: 60-6311, 36-1311, 36-1868, 36-1226, 36-1436

- **Established:** April 27, 1965

- **Organization:** The *Universidad Santa María La Antigua* is the most prestigious private university in Panama. It offers both first university degree and *maestría* level programs. Undergraduate programs consist of 16-week semesters, with each class period lasting 50 minutes. On the graduate level, there are quarters of 14 weeks, and class periods of 60 minutes.

  The *USMA* is licensed to operate and is recognized by the Ministry of Education. The university designs its own programs and does not have to receive the approval of the other public universities or any governmental body.

- **Admission:** The *bachiller* or secondary school diploma, plus an admission examination, are required for matriculation.

- **Grading Scale:** Grades range from 0 to 3, as follows:

Points	Description	Letter Grade	Grade Points
91-100	Excellent (*Sobresaliente*)	A	3
81-90	Good (*Bueno*)	B	2
71-80	Average (*Regular*)	C	1
61-70	Passing (*Mínimo*)	D	0
0-60	Failing (*Fracaso*)	F	0
	No Grade (*Sin Nota*)	S.N.	
	Incomplete (*Incompleto*)	I	

Academic indexes: averages of 1.00 to 1.74 are considered to be a C average; 1.75 to 2.49 are B; and 2.5 to 3.0 are A. Those graduating with the following averages receive the indicated notation on their academic records:

2.50- 2.69	*cum laude*
2.70- 2.89	*magna cum laude*
2.90- 3.00	*summa cum laude*

Universidad Tecnológica de Panamá/UTP (Technological University of Panama)
Apdo. 6-2894
El Dorado

- **Enrollment:** Approximately 9,500

- **Academic calendar:** Two 16-week semesters and a summer session

- **Organization:** The university has numerous regional centers throughout Panama, including Bocas del Toro, Los Santos, Coclé, Chorrera, Chiriquí, Colón, and Veraguas.

- **Grading Scale:** 0 to 100, as follows:

Score	Grade	Index	Description (Translation)
91-100	A	3	*Sobresaliente* (Outstanding)
81-90	B	2	*Bueno* (Good)
71-80	C	1	*Regular* (Average)
61-70	D	0	*Deficiente* (Poor)
0-60	F	0	*Fracasado* (Failing)

The minimum passing grade in a course is a "D." Students who receive a grade of "D" may repeat the course. Students who receive a grade of "F" in a course must repeat it and pass with a grade of at least a "C." Students must maintain a cumulative grade point average of greater than one (1) to remain in good academic standing. If a student passes a course with a "C" or better in another institution or department of the university, the word *Acreditada* (credited) appears instead of a letter grade.

On the postgraduate level, students must maintain at least a 1.5 cumulative grade point average to remain in good standing and a minimum of 2.0 average to graduate. Postgraduate (*maestría*) students may also receive grades of Incomplete (*Incompleto* or I), or Withdrawn (*Retirado* or R) which indicates that the student was given permission by the professor to withdraw from the course without a grade.

The university calculates its credit system based on the total number of credit hours a student takes per semester. Each credit hour equals 1 hour per week of class or seminar time, or 2 or 3 hours of laboratory time or practical training. Unlike most other institutions, *UTP* does not require a thesis for completion of its undergraduate programs.

UTP offers academic programs in the following (colleges) *facultades*: (See Documents 8.2 and 8.3)

Civil Engineering
Computer Systems Engineering
Industrial Engineering
Mechanical Engineering
Systems Engineering

Other Institutions:

Instituto Superior de Administración de Empresas/ISAE (Higher Institution of Business Administration)

• **Established** and authorized to grant degrees: June 1994
Programs of study include Business Administration, Marketing, and General Accounting.

Florida State University
Panama Canal Branch
Albrook
Unit 0922
APO AA 34002
Tel.: 86-4470, 27-4661
Ft. Davis
Unit 1518
APO AA 34005
Tel.: 89-3537

• **Organization:** The FSU Panama Canal Branch grants bachelor's degrees in computer science, international affairs, Latin American and Caribbean Studies (LACS), LACS/Business, Social Science and Spanish. The program is administered by a director at Albrook Air Force Station. Classes are taught in English by resident fulltime faculty. The branch is recognised by the Southern Association of Colleges and Schools as a degree-granting institution.

Panama Canal College
Department of Defense Dependents Schools
Panama Region
APO
Miami, Florida 34002

• **Organization:** Panama Canal College's predecessor, Canal Zone Junior College, opened in 1933. Its contemporary successor operates like a U.S community college, with all instruction in English. The College grants associate degrees to Panamanian residents; programs require 64 semester-hour credits.

Glossary:

Abogado(a). Lawyer

Acreditada . Granted credit

Aprobado(a). Passed

Arquitecto(a). Architect

Bachillerato or *bachiller.* Secondary school diploma

Carrera. Program of study/major/specialization

Cirujano Dentista. Dental Surgeon

Doctor/Doctorado. Doctor, usually of medicine or dentistry (a first university degree in Central America); also may be a graduate level doctorate in philosophy, a credential that is emerging in Central American higher education.

Especialización. Specialization
Fracasado. Failed

Ingeniero(a)/Ingeniería. Engineer(ing)

Licenciado(a)/Licenciatura. Licentiate, generally first university degree

Maestría. Master's

Maestro/a . Teacher

Pensum. List of required courses and prerequisites for a specific program; also called *plan de estudios* (study plan)

Perito. Expert, may be a secondary-level credential

Profesorado. Teaching degree

Profesor(a) en (specialization). Teacher of (specialization)

Reprobado(a). Failed

Técnico en. Technician in (specialization)

Título. Title/ degree

UNIVERSIDAD LATINA

No. ░░░░░

REGISTRO DE CALIFICACIONES

FECHA: 5 DE MAYO DE 1994   PAGINA: 1

CIEN. ADMI.Y ECONOMICAS
LICENCIATURA EN ADMINISTRACION
ENFASIS EN CONTABILIDAD
░░░░░   ░░░░░ ░░░░░   2-121-920

AÑO	CUATR.	NOMBRE DEL CURSO	CREDI.	NOTAS
1992	1	CONTABILIDAD I	4	92.00
1992	1	ADMINISTRACION	4	95.00
1992	1	MATEMATICA I	4	CONV.
1992	1	INGLES I	4	CONV.
1993	2	CONTABILIDAD II	4	91.00
1993	2	ADM. RECURSOS HUMANOS	4	95.95
1993	2	MATEMATICA FINANCIERA	4	99.00
1993	2	INGLES II	4	100.00
1993	3	CONTABILIDAD III	4	99.00
1993	3	ESTADISTICA I	4	88.00
1993	3	COMPUTACION	4	99.00
1993	3	CALCULO ADUANAL	4	97.00
1993	4	CONTABILIDAD IV	4	79.00
1993	4	DERECHO MERCANTIL	4	96.00
1993	4	ESTADISTICA II	4	92.00
1993	4	MICROECONOMIA	4	88.00
1994	5	CONTABILIDAD DE COSTOS I	4	100.00

NOTA: ESTE DOCUMENTO SOLO ES VALIDO CON EL SELLO DE LA UNIVERSIDAD Y LA FIRMA DEL DIRECTOR.

Document 8.1a The Panamanian branch of the *Universidad Latina* (Latin University) of Costa Rica operates on a quarterly system ("cuatr.")

UNIVERSIDAD LATINA

No. 000087

REGISTRO DE CALIFICACIONES

FECHA: 5 DE MAYO DE 1994   PAGINA: 2

CIEN. ADMI.Y ECONOMICAS
LICENCIATURA EN ADMINISTRACION
ENFASIS EN CONTABILIDAD
_____   _____   2-121-920

ANO	CUATR.	NOMBRE DEL CURSO	CREDI.	NOTAS
1994	5	MERCADEO I	4	96.00
1994	5	MACROECONOMIA	4	93.00
1994	5	DERECHO LABORAL	4	85.00

SU INDICE ACUMULATIVO ES....... 93.61
TOTAL CREDITOS....... 80

DIRECTORA EJECUTIVA: _____
                    por ZONIA G. DE SMITH

NOTA: ESTE DOCUMENTO SOLO ES VALIDO CON EL SELLO DE LA UNIVERSIDAD Y LA FIRMA DEL DIRECTOR.

Document 8.1b (see previous)

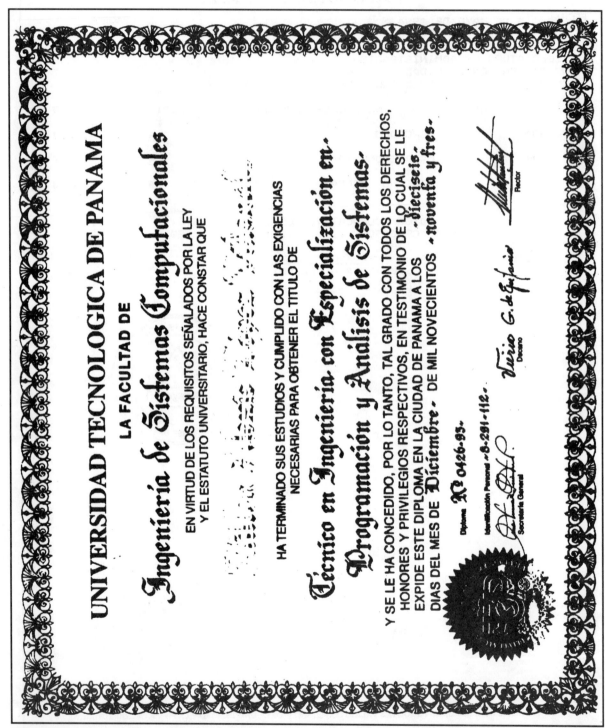

Document 8.2 *Técnico* diploma from the Engineering schools of the *Universidad Tecnológica de Panama*/UTP (Technological University of Panama).

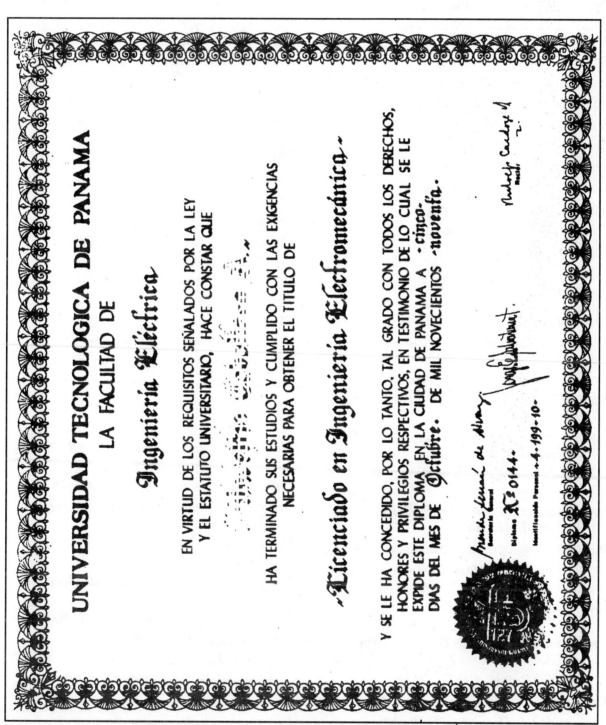

Document 8.3 *Licenciado* diploma from the Engineering schools of the *Universidad Tecnológica*.

Institutional Listing, By Country

National Council on the Evaluation of Foreign Educational Credentials and the Placement Recommendations in this Workshop Report

The placement recommendations published in this PIER workshop report have been approved by the National Council on the Evaluation of Foreign Educational Credentials (the Council) in consultation with the authors. The Council was established to provide guidance concerning foreign educational credentials to U.S. institutions of higher education. It is the only inter-associational body in the United States specifically organized to perform this role.

The membership of the Council reflects the diversity of U.S. educational institutions for which placement recommendations are made. The member organizations are the American Association of Community Colleges (AACC), the American Association of Collegiate Registrars and Admissions Officers (AACRAO), the American Council on Education (ACE), The College Board, the Council of Graduate Schools (CGS), the Institute of International Education (IIE), and NAFSA: Association of International Educators. Observers from U.S. organizations interested in international education include the United States Information Agency (USIA), the Agency for International Development (AACRAO-AID), and the New York State Education Department. Their representatives for 1993-1995 are listed below.

Members of the National Council on the Evaluation of Foreign Educational Credentials:

Chair: Karen Lukas, Assistant Director of Admissions, University of Minnesota-Twin Cities, Minneapolis, MN (AACRAO)

Chair Elect: Robert K. Brashear, Director of Admissions, Graduate School, Cornell University-Ithaca, NY (AACRAO)

AACC-James Mahoney, Director, Administration, AACC, Washington, DC
AACRAO-William H. Smart, Director of Sponsored Student Programs, International Education, Oregon State University, Corvallis, OR (Chair of PIER)
ACE-Barbara Turlington, Director, International Education, ACE, Washington, DC
The College Board-Marcelle Heerschap, Director, Office of Admissions, The American University, Washington, DC

CGS-James Siddens, Assistant Dean, Graduate School, Ohio State University, Columbus, OH
IIE-Nicole Morgenstern, Director, Placement and Special Services Division, IIE, New York, NY
NAFSA-Margarita Sianou, World Education Services, Inc., New York, NY; Ellen Silverman, University Admissions Processing Center/CUNY, Brooklyn, NY; Robert Watkins, Assistant Director of Admissions, University of Texas at Austin, Austin, TX

Representatives from Observer Organizations:

AACRAO-AID-Dale Gough, Director, AACRAO-AID/Office of International Education, Services, Washington, DC
NY State Education Department-Susan Fuller, Credentials Assessment, State Education Department, Albany, NY

(Order by telephone, fax, or mail with form on next page)

World Education Series (WES) Publications *(member/non-member price)*

Full Country Studies

Argentina (1993) by Liz Reisberg. 248pp. $30/$45

Australia (1983) by Caroline Aldrich-Langen. 276pp. $8/$12

Belgium (1985) by Ann Fletcher. 192pp. $8/$12

Colombia (1984) by Stanley Wellington. 144pp. $8/$12

Denmark (1995) by Valerie A. Woolston and Karlene N. Dickey. 162pp. $35/$50

Dominican Republic (1987) by Kathleen Sellew. 136pp. $8/$12

Egypt (1988) by Lee Wilcox. 112pp. $15/$20

Federal Republic of Germany (1986) by Georgeanne Porter. 192pp. $15/$20

France (1988) by Mariam Assefa. 252pp. $15/$20

Indonesia (1993) by Karin Johnson, Gerald Chamberland, and Wendy Gaylor. 192pp. $40/$60

Iraq (1988) by James Frey. 192pp. $15/$20

Japan (1989) by Ellen Mashiko. 176pp. $20/$25

Malaysia (1986) by Joann Stedman. 184pp. $15/$20

Mexico (1982) by Kitty Villa. 288pp. $8/$12

The Netherlands (1984) by Peter Schuler. 208pp. $8/$12

New Zealand (1981) by Patrick Kennedy. 96pp. $8/$12

Norway (1994) by Shelley M. Feagles and Karlene N. Dickey. 176pp. $35/$50

Peru (1983) by Colleen Gray. 132pp. $8/$12

Sweden (1995) by Kathleen T. Zanotti and Karlene M. Dickey. 192pp. $35/$50

Workshop Reports

The Admission and Placement of Students from Bahrain, Oman, Qatar, United Arab Emirates, and Yemen Arab Republic (1984). J.K. Johnson (ed.). 114pp. $7.95/$20

The Admission and Placement of Students from Bangladesh, India, Pakistan, and Sri Lanka (1986) by Leo J. Sweeney and Valerie Woolston (eds.). 370pp. $10.95/$25

Bulgaria; A Study of the Educational System and Guide to the Placement of Students in Educational Institutions in the United States (1995) Margery Ismail (Dir.), Arunas Alisauskas (Asso. Dir. and Co-Ed.), and Caroline Aldrich-Langen (Co-Ed.) 96pp. $35/50

The Admission and Placement of Students from Canada (1989) James S. Frey (ed.). 560pp. $35/50

The Admission and Placement of Students from Central America (1988). Caroline Aldrich-Langen and Kathleen Sellew (eds.). 236pp. $12/25

The Admission and Placement of Students from the Czech and Slovak Federal Republic (1992). Edward Devlin (ed.). 142pp. $25/$40

The Admission and Placement of Students from the Republic of Hungary (1990) Karlene N. Dickey and Desmond Bevis (eds.). 128pp. $15/$30

The Admission and Placement of Students from the Republic of Poland (1992). Edward Devlin (ed.). 176pp. $30/$45

The Admission and Placement of Students from Yugoslavia (1990). Karlene N. Dickey and Desmond Bevis (eds.). 112pp. $15/$30

The Educational System of the United Kingdom: The Admission and Placement of Students from the United Kingdom and Study Abroad Opportunities (1990). Sylvia Higashi and Alan Margolis (eds.). 240pp. $25/$40

Special Reports

The Educational System of Australia: An Update of the 1983 World Education Series Volume (1990) by Caroline Aldrich-Langen. 74pp. $12

Central America Update (1996) by Jane E. Marcus. 136pp. $20/35

Education on the Island of Cyprus (1990) by Margit Schatzman. 65pp. $10

The Educational System of the Former German Democratic Republic (1991) by Karen Lukas. 80pp. $15/$20

Higher Education in Israel (1993) by Ann Fletcher. 56pp. $15/$25

New Independent States & The Baltic Republics: A Directory of Institutions of Higher Education in Armenia, Azerbaijan, Belarus, Estonia, Georgia, Kazakhstan, Kyrgyzstan, Latvia, Lithuania, Moldova, Russia, Tajikistan, Turkmenistan, Ukraine, Uzbekistan (1995) by Erika Popovych. 458pp. w/binder $35/$50.

Postsecondary Institutions of the People's Republic of China: A Comprehensive Guide to Institutions of Higher Education (1992) by William Paver and Yipin Wan. 625pp. $35/$50

The Soviet System of Education (1992) by Erika Popovych and Brian Levin-Stankevich. 144pp. $25/$40

Swiss Higher Schools of Engineering and Swiss Higher Schools of Economics and Business Administration (1991) by Karlene N. Dickey and Karen Lukas. 68pp. $15/$20

Understanding the Admissions Process in U.S. Higher Education: A Study Approach (1993) by Caroline Aldrich-Langen. 36pp. $15/$25

Working Papers

Guide to Placement Recommendations (1992) by the National Council on the Evaluation of Foreign Educational Credentials. 12pp. $6

The Kuwait System of Education (1993) by Ismail Safwat. 36pp. $15/$25

Methods and Skills for Research in Foreign Educational Systems: A Report on the 1994 NAFSA/ EAIE Seminars (1995) by Caroline Aldrich-Langen. 60pp. $10/15

A Study of the Educational System of the Republic of Slovenia (1995) by Karlene N. Dickey. 127pp. $15/25

Other Publications

For information about out-of-print WES publications and other international resources contact AACRAO at (202) 293-9161 or NAFSA at (202) 462-4811.

Publications Order Form for Photocopying

Indispensable for anyone interested in international education or the evaluation of foreign credentials

Take advantage of these special prices while supplies last.

...call 301 317 6588 or photocopy and mail this order form to:

PIER Publications
P.O. Box 231
Annapolis Junction, MD 20701
TEL: 301 317 6588   FAX: 301 206 9789

Send Invoice To:	**Ship To (if different from invoice):**
Name _____	Name _____
Institution _____	Institution _____
Address _____	Address _____
City _____	City _____
State _____ Zip _____	State _____ Zip _____
Phone Number _____	Phone Number _____

NEW!   #5325 Central America Update   #5338 Bulgaria   #5339 Romania

#5344 Methods and Skills for Research in Foreign Educational Systems

#5345 New Independent States   #5343 Republic of Slovenia

1995 SCANDINAVIAN SERIES (regularly $35 each, all 3 for $90)

#5335 Norway   #5337 Sweden   #5336 Denmark

Other Publications included in this special offer: (only $25 each for any 4 or more)*

__#5309 Indonesia __#5319 China (a directory of institutions)
__#5301 Argentina __#5327 Hungary
__#5328 Poland __#5333 Canada
__#5334 Mexico __#5326 Czech & Slovak Republics
__#5320 Soviet System __#5331 United Kingdom
__#5329 (former) Yugoslavia   (use "√" for choices, "x" for alternates)

Please send me the above marked items, or other (from preceding page) _____

TOTAL ORDER (items x $=) $ _____   Plus Shipping $_____ = $_____

Shipping Rate Information:

AMOUNT	U.S., CANADA	OTHER COUNTRIES
Under $25	$3.50	$5.00
$25-$50	$5.00	$7.5
Over $50	10%	15%

Federal Express Account # for quick delivery: _____

_____ AACRAO Member _____ NAFSA Member _____ Other
_____ MasterCard _____ VISA _____ American Express
_____ Check or money order enclosed

Credit card number # _____ expiration date _____
(Signature) _____

*Rates offered in this special promotion are for a limited time only